# THE RENFREW MILLIONAIRES

## THE VALLEY BOYS OF WINTER 1910

*Frank Cosentino*

GSPH

Published by

GSPH  GENERAL STORE
       PUBLISHING HOUSE

1 Main Street, Burnstown, Ontario, Canada K0J 1G0
Telephone  (613)432-7697  Fax (613)432-7184

ISBN 0-919431-35-6
Printed and bound in Canada.

Cover Design and Layout - Hugh Malcolm, Marlene McRoberts, Bill Slavin

Copyright ©1990
The General Store Publishing House Inc.
Burnstown, Ontario, Canada



Due to the historical nature of this manuscript it has been decided to retain the
imperial measurements.

General Store Publishing House Inc. gratefully acknowledges the
assistance of the Ontario Arts Council.

**Canadian Cataloguing in Publication Data**

Cosentino, Frank, 1937-
  Renfrew Millionaires: the valley boys of winter 1910

  ISBN 0-919431-35-6

    1. Renfrew Millionaires (hockey team) --History.
I.  Title.

GV848.R46C68 1990   796.96'2'0971381   C90-090294-9

First Printing October 1990
Second Printing July 1994

To the Valley Boys in my life: Amby, Charlie, Clarence, John, John, Kevin, Les, Lorne, Fr. Louis, Fr. Mike and Weck.

# Table Of Contents

# *Introduction*

The Renfrew Millionaires represent the end of an era in hockey history. The 1910 season was the last hurrah of that period; Renfrew was the last of the small towns to have embarked on a civic crusade to win the Stanley Cup.

Hockey has been described as the Canadian Specific. With the introduction of the Stanley Cup in 1893, many towns across the young country sought to define themselves, inwardly and to the outside world, as Stanley Cup champions.

Through its trustees, Cup challenges were entertained from all parts of the Dominion, from all sizes of communities: Montreal, Winnipeg, Ottawa, Vancouver, Edmonton, Toronto and Halifax, vied with Rat Portage, Dawson, New Glasgow and Galt. The smaller communities had always attempted to pick up one or two established players in an attempt to wrest the trophy from the holders. The Renfrew team of 1910 represents the greatest example of that. It was a collection of veritable all-stars from across the country, all attracted by the huge money being offered by Renfrew millionaire M.J. O'Brien and, of course, by their love for the game.

After 1910, Renfrew was to continue for one more season in the National Hockey Association - a league it helped to form -

with a much diminished line-up. Changes had occurred. Challenges became progressively more limited to the top professional leagues as limitations were being placed on players travelling from one club to another. The National Hockey Association, later the National Hockey League, and the Pacific Coast Hockey Association virtually tied up all challenges to the Cup as their league schedules lengthened. Once the PCHA dropped out of hockey, the Stanley Cup became the sole province of the NHL.

Beginning in the 1911 season, the owners of the various teams in the NHA banded together to impose more control over the game, its players and the challenges for the Stanley Cup. To restrict the free movement of the players, clubs moved from verbal agreements, as Ottawa had always operated with, to the written contract (see appendix B).

The contract was described as "iron bound, steel inset and unbreakable."[1] The player was "tied up in knots,"[2] by the league. It was an abrupt change from the "loose methods employed by the professional clubs in previous years when players were permitted to hold down big salaries and jump from one team to another or one league to another without molestation or interference,"[3] from the club or league where they were employed.

Not only were players tied up for the current season with their team, they could not "join any other club even at the expiration of the contract without first securing their release from the club in whose employ they now are."[4] The players were unhappy; the contract was as "unpopular as is Jack Johnson in the State of California. . . worse than a life sentence."[5]

But during the 1910 season, there was none of that. Life was simpler; it was the year of the Creamery Kings, the boys from Butterville, from O'Brienville, the Valley Boys, Renfrew's Boys of Winter, the Millionaires.

# Chapter One

*Odds and Ends, Here and There and the Stanley Cup.*

It was a late-autumn day, that November in 1909, when J. Ambrose O'Brien sat in his construction office in La Tuque. The phone rang. It was one of the Barnets, Jim, from Renfrew.[1] The two had a common interest. They were both sons of millionaires but they had a passion, hockey. They longed for the day when Renfrew would challenge for and win the Stanley Cup. Now Jim was telling Ambrose of a meeting in Montreal to form a new hockey league. The hockey promised to be the finest anywhere. Would Ambrose take the train to Montreal to see if Renfrew could join?

O'Brien stifled an urge to tell Barnet that he was crazy. After all, having been away from Renfrew for the last few years attending university in Toronto, he had seen those big-city men operate, but hockey was in his blood. He had played junior, intermediate and senior hockey in Renfrew as well as intercollegiate with the University of Toronto. Instead, he thought of the prize, swallowed hard, put all his doubts aside, and agreed. He would journey to Montreal. It was a journey that would propel the small Ottawa Valley town of Renfrew into hockey history.

In 1909, Renfrew was a farming community, situated in the Ottawa Valley, noted especially for its creamery where top-grade butter was churned out. The town took great pride in its thoroughly modern process which gave it a well deserved reputation throughout the valley. Competitors' products were dealt with harshly: "A rose by any other name may smell as sweet but conversely, neither the smell nor the taste of axle grease is improved by labelling it 'creamery butter.'"[2] The population of Renfrew was approximately three thousand, mostly Scottish, with a healthy number of Irish and pockets of German, Polish and French. Farming was the main occupation but if the town's reputation was earned because of its creamery, it was enhanced by its hockey teams' successes and the "fairy godfather of Renfrew,"[3] M.J. O'Brien. The three ingredients combined to give us a unique picture of one of Canada's legends in her sporting history.

**The Stanley Cup**

It is a credit to Governor General Lord Stanley and his British public-school educational background that he recognized the unique attraction of hockey on ice. As a keen athlete in his native England, he had played a variety of sports and was familiar with the lessons of life to be learned on the playing fields as well as the joy experienced through effort. He became quite a follower of the hockey scene in Ottawa and what's more, supervised the erecting of a large outdoor rink at Rideau Hall, the official residence of the Governor General. There, he agreed to the formation of the Rideau Hall Rebels. Included among the red-shirted team members were two of Lord Stanley's sons, Algernon and Arthur. It was a classic case of nineteenth-century gentility. The hockey was really an opportunity for a social occasion. Playing with members of parliament or teams in far away Toronto, there were always tea and crumpets available and much social chit-chat. Indeed, there was so much enthusiasm about the game that even when Lord Stanley returned to England, having satisfied his term of office, his five sons introduced the game to Britain when they played a Palace team on a frozen lake on the grounds of Buckingham Palace.[4]

Before he left Ottawa, Lord Stanley decided to do something to encourage the sport he had come to love - and to recognize the team he thought to be so great, the Ottawas. The Lord Stanley Cup was to be presented to the "leading hockey club in Canada."[5] It was to be a challenge trophy with the trustees, Sheriff Sweetland and P.D. Ross, two Ottawa sportsmen, having the responsibility of determining the team that would have its challenge recognized. The trustees were zealous in their impartiality. When the Ottawa Club of 1892/93, as champions of their league, declared that they should be awarded the Cup, the trustees, as previously mentioned both Ottawa men, informed them that they would have to play Osgoode Hall. Not only that, the game would have to be played in Toronto! Ottawa refused. The trustees insisted! The stalemate continued, long after the thaw melted the ice of the outdoor rinks. Finally, the trustees declared that the Montreal Amateur Athletic Association was the first to hold the Stanley Cup.

Their first defence of the symbol came in 1894, when, on March 22, five thousand spectators saw the Stanley Cup champions retain the Cup by defeating Ottawa by a 3-1 score. Unfortunately, Lord Stanley saw neither this nor any other Stanley Cup game. Nonetheless, hockey grew in popularity and the Stanley Cup became a symbol much coveted. More and more towns and cities sought to win the trophy, by now a national quest, east, west, north and south. Teams from Dawson, Rat Portage, New Glasgow, Berlin and Galt as well as from larger cities such as Montreal, Ottawa, Winnipeg and Edmonton spared no effort in trying to be hailed as Stanley Cup champions.

Like most sport in Canada in the late-nineteenth century and the early twentieth, amateur hockey held sway. After all, amateurism was a nineteenth-century British concept; Canada was a British colony. Whatever was in vogue in the mother country was steadfastly followed in the Dominion. And so it was that hockey in its infancy was a game for amateurs which by this time meant that it was played without recompense. Amateurism was the acceptable code. If one were shown to have accepted money for sport, you were declared a professional[6] and in the late-nineteenth century there were few worse names that a player could be called. Amateur and sportsman were synonymous. The professional was the odd man out, barred for life from amateur sport if it was proven that he accepted money for playing - and amateur sport was the only game in town! Shortly after the turn of the century, however, a combination of factors caused conditions to be changed. Artificial ice made its appearance in Pittsburgh. With ice incorporated into an arena, Canadian hockey players were being lured to the Steel City for thirty dollars per week. Not only that, because the season was being extended since it was no longer dependent upon the weather, the players were willing to ignore the amateur restrictions; they could earn more money because there were more games and, even more so, could exhibit their skills before an appreciative, if less sophisticated, hockey audience.

In Houghton, Michigan, a mining community of thirty-five hundred, the first league to declare itself openly professional was formed in 1904. Its founder was a Canadian, J.L. Gibson, a dentist who had been declared a professional in 1897 when he played with the Berlin club. Moving to the Michigan town, he suggested that the hockey team should look to Canada with its abundance of good players. The Ontario Hockey Association reacted sternly: "Keep away from Houghton or Pittsburgh or you go into the darkness of professionalism."[7] A few years earlier, this might have been enough to discourage movement from the "light" of amateurism. But that was when there were no options available for the athletes to pursue. The more these bold new ventures of artificial ice and professional leagues were visible, the more they caught the fancy of the public and lessened the players' fears of moving into the "darkness."

Lacrosse players and teams were already coming to grips with the new reality and by 1906, hockey was too. The Stanley Cup was the impetus. It had been proven that good players would move should it be made worth their while financially. And to win the Cup you needed good players! Promoters of the game asserted that the public didn't care whether a player was amateur or professional "as long as he can deliver the goods. To get good hockey we have to pay the players."[8] That sentiment was put into practice when yet another league declared itself openly professional. This one included Guelph, St. Catharines, Berlin, Galt, Brantford and Toronto. So sure was it that it would be accepted by the public that it named itself the Ontario Professional Hockey League, later better known as the Trolley League. Guelph and St. Catharines were to fold before the season finished, their players dispersed among the other teams. Nonetheless, pro hockey had been accepted.

Enough clubs felt this in 1907 that a rival athletic federation, led by the Montreal Amateur Athletic Association, broke away from the CAAU in what was termed the Athletic War. The new Amateur Athletic Federation allowed professionals to mix with amateurs as long as they declared themselves. Legitimacy was now given to a practice which had become more commonplace as the years unfolded. By 1908, the "darkness" was all but dispelled. Stanley Cup trustee William Foran (he was from Ottawa and had replaced Sheriff Sweetland) stated emphatically: "The Stanley Cup is not hung up for either amateur or professional hockey in particular but for the best hockey."[9] That was all that was needed. The Stanley Cup was fair game. The stage was set for the "fairy godfather of Renfrew,"[10] M.J. O'Brien.

To all who followed the popular winter pastime, the best hockey was played from Ottawa to Montreal (at least that's what people from Ottawa and Montreal felt). Those two cities alternated with each other as Stanley Cup champions with only occasional interruptions from Winnipeg or Rat Portage.

It was probably in 1907 that Renfrew's dreams of a Stanley Cup were spawned. In that year they were champions of the

Upper Ottawa Valley League and defeated Van Kleek Hill, winners of the Lower Ottawa Valley League. They were awarded the Citizen Shield, the trophy given by the Ottawa newspaper and described as the "Stanley Cup of the Ottawa Valley."[11] But what really got them thinking about the real Stanley Cup was when they played and defeated the real Stanley Cup champions, the legendary Ottawa Silver Seven. Sure it was only an exhibition game, but the score was 9-5; Renfrew had shown that they could play with the big boys. In Ottawa there was only derision. Their team didn't want to go all out, they said. There was no sense in insulting a small town. The game needed all the fans it could gather throughout the Valley.

In Renfrew, excitement built. The Stanley Cup, fast becoming the nation's elixir to a cold winter, was within its grasp, certainly within its capability. Team officials prepared to challenge the Montreal Wanderers, the holders of the Cup. The trustees were not convinced. Renfrew's league, they pronounced, was not on a par with the Eastern Canada Hockey Association which housed the Ottawa and Montreal teams. The Toronto *Telegram* mocked the Renfrew challenge for the Stanley Cup "all because they won a fence-corner league." It went on to advise its readers to refrain from laughing ". . . if you never lived in a country town, you don't know how seriously these people take themselves."[12] And indeed, they did take themselves seriously. J.G. Barnet, the president of the Renfrew club and son of Alexander Barnet, a Renfrew millionaire, enlisted the help of the fairy godfather, M.J. O'Brien.

A self-made man, O'Brien was born in Nova Scotia in 1851. When his father met with an accident and was unable to work, O'Brien was employed as a fifteen-year-old water-boy on the Truro-to-Pictou railroad line in Nova Scotia. His pay was ten cents per pail. Soon he was able to buy a horse and hire a man. He became a foreman at eighteen and one year later, a subcontractor. Going down the road to Ontario, he decided to bid on the last leg of the railway being proposed from Kingston to Pembroke, the K and P, better known perhaps as the Kick and Push. As he was walking the land through which the railroad would be built, he came to a clearing at Calabogie. There he met Jenny Barry. They later married and settled in Renfrew which was to serve as his home base for his expanding business involvements.[13] O'Brien soon became a millionaire engaged in mining for gold, silver, cobalt and nickel, a timberman, an industrialist, and an owner of woollen mills and munition plants. Indeed there didn't seem to be much that O'Brien wasn't involved in. He seemed to have his finger in every pie, determined to show that Renfrew, in spite of its small rural population of around three thousand, had as much to offer as any town in the country.

When *The Renfrew Journal* reported in 1907, "there will be no Stanley Cup this year," it placed the blame on "soft ice and admitted hard luck."[14] When Renfrew had made an application to the trustees to challenge for the Cup, they were told by the Ottawa men that they should play the Ottawa Victorias (so many teams in different cities seemed to be called the Victorias in honour of the admired Queen) in a two-game, total-goal series, the winner to challenge the Montreal Wanderers, holders of the Cup. There was no question among the Ottawa fans as to who were their favourites. Large bursts of applause greeted the Victorias every time they touched the puck; restrained enthusiasm was reserved for the Renfrew team as they made a play which had been thought to be above their capability. Horace Gaul of Renfrew played with his head bandaged; the Ottawa patrons seemed to be particularly appreciative of his plucky work as they cheered him every time that he touched the puck. Ottawa defeated Renfrew by a 4-1 score to lead the two-game round by three goals. The following Monday, at the Argyle Street rink in Renfrew, the return contest was played. Now it was the local fans' turn to show their support. Fully half of the town's population, some seventeen hundred spectators, jammed the rink. Some had come to see if Fred Taylor, the Cyclone from Listowel who had been playing in the International League, would be in Renfrew's line-up. The rumour had begun circulating that he was offered fifteen hundred dollars, an unheard-of figure, to join Renfrew for the return game and the 1908 season. It was the first of many rumours, over the next three years, concerning Taylor, Renfrew and Ottawa.

Taylor did not join Renfrew for the Ottawa game, the *Mercury* reporting, "his reputation for backbone has not been enhanced by the affair."[15] The *Journal* confided that the fifteen hundred dollar offer "will give our readers an idea of the magnitude of the financial operations in big-game hockey."[16] Indeed, it was a serious pursuit; at times there seemed to be a take-no-prisoners approach to the game. In one incident in the return match, Steve Vair of Renfrew hit Charles Ross of Ottawa with his stick causing the loss of four teeth and a cut needing four stitches. Recovering from the momentary shock, Ross made a dash for Vair, knocked him to the ground and began to pummel him. Both were assessed ten minutes "behind the hockey bars."[17] The game was tense, fraught with excitement. Moving into a 3-1 lead, Renfrew came so close to scoring the fourth and tying goal of the series that "some staid old men from Burnstown, shall we say - did jump and shout encouragement to the Renfrew players." The "momentous game" and "splendid effort"[18] went by all too quickly. Yet the evidence was there for all to see. Renfrew could compete with its bigger rival, Ottawa. The lesson was not lost.

Yet another millionaire, Alexander Barnet, a Renfrew lumber baron and industrialist, was attracted by the possibility of Renfrew gaining much widespread recognition if they won the Stanley Cup. The two men provided financial backing for Renfrew's entry into a new league, the Federal. There were two reasons why Renfrew moved to the new league. Firstly, both Ottawa and the Montreal Wanderers had withdrawn from the Federal and moved to the Eastern Canada Amateur Hockey Association. Included in this league were Ottawa, the Wanderers, the Montreal Shamrocks, Quebec and the

Montreal Victorias. Ottawa had just built a new arena on Laurier Avenue. A seating capacity of forty-five hundred and standing room for an additional twenty-five hundred made it a huge facility. Top competition was called for in every game in order to make a profit. Secondly, it was becoming obvious that the money needed to ice a team was beyond a small rink's capacity. Ottawa had tried to coax Tom Phillips, described as the best player in the game, to play with them for eighteen hundred dollars, a mind-boggling amount for the average follower and player of 1908. Other Ottawa players were signed for cash or given stock in the club.

Renfrew stepped gingerly into this scene when it played Pembroke of the Upper Ottawa Valley League in an exhibition. The two Valley teams were natural rivals to begin with but when Renfrew took to the ice in December of 1907 with Ernie Liffiton of the Montreal Wanderers in its line-up, Pembroke objected. They refused to take to the ice. Renfrew countered that Pembroke had a number of Ottawa players with its team. Charges flew back and forth; tempers were elevated in the stands and on the ice. Finally at 9 pm, Pembroke agreed to play. It might have been that the two teams had already agreed to play the next game in Pembroke, before what would be the largest crowd of the season, suitably exercised. The more likely reason however was that in reality there was never any doubt that the game would be played. There was just too much money at stake! There was a public fetish for gambling. Side-bets between Renfrew and Pembroke followers were plentiful. Club owners would put up a money purse to go to the winner of the game or the bet. Almost any variety of bet was available: the number of goals scored, the difference between the teams in goals, the number scored in each half, the difference taking into account the handicap given. Thus there would be a lot of preliminary investigating and scouting done of the competition. Who were their players? What were their weaknesses? How did our strengths stack up against their weaknesses? Where would be the best place to move the puck? Before one agreed to a bet, one liked to think that there would be no surprises. Everything had been taken into account based on past knowledge. In this particular game, it appeared as if Renfrew had pulled a fast one. But hope springs eternal. Even when they were ahead by a 3-0 count at the half, "a Pembroke blood offered $150 at even money (that Pembroke would win) and of course was covered."[19] *The Ottawa Free Press* reported that the supply of money the visitors had on hand, and were willing to bet "at evens" was evidence of Pembroke's confidence. "The betting in towns up this way," it continued, "somewhat belittles the wagering in Ottawa and Montreal. A roll of three or four hundred dollars is put up and covered with no further ado. Small bets are scoffed at."[20]

Both teams agreed to a rematch in Pembroke set for January 17, 1908. The Pembroke *Observer* fuelled the flames even more by describing Renfrew as a circus town, "the side show in the hockey league." It accused Renfrew of trying to pose as a hockey threat when all fans knew that "Montreal, Ottawa and Barrie and other places hold the laurels."[21]

Renfrew took to the ice amid a chorus of boos and catcalls. Pembroke appeared buoyed by the sustained cheering of its fans who increased their volume when they recognized three members of the Montreal Wanderers skating with the home team. No ordinary members either. These three were established pros: Art Ross, Charlie Chipchase and Tom Hooper. The Renfrew players skated over to their bench to await instructions. After all, there were a lot of bets at stake. About one hundred Renfrewites had made the trip not only to see a good hockey game but to, just as importantly, add to their cash holdings. The air turned tense; fears of a riot were surfacing.

It was 9:30 before the contest began. It did not end until 12:30 in the morning. Disputes were continuous; every stoppage in play produced more and more wrangling. Pembroke followers were becoming more and more restless as their fear of becoming separated from their money approached reality. It appeared that the officials were desperate to have the Pembroke/Wanderers combination win. For a seemingly innocent infraction, Spittal of Renfrew was penalized; the Pembroke team failed to score. Just as Spittal was released from his penalty and about to step on the ice, he was arrested by Constable Dickson of Pembroke and not allowed to continue. Pandemonium broke out but the Constable was adamant; Spittal could not continue. He was to be locked up for the night.

When all was said and done, Renfrew won the contest by an 8-6 score but the match and its incidents did not escape the Ottawa and Toronto newspapers. The *Citizen* quoted Eddie Phillips, the referee, as saying: "Spittal played a remarkably clean game," was ruled off just once, the time he was arrested. "The entire trouble," the paper continued, "was originated and sustained by the gambling element as he termed the sports who put money on teams." Pembroke contended that Eddie Phillips was a robber. Pronounced *The Globe*: "These are the regular accompaniments of the OVL games which seem to run for the cheap gamblers that follow them."[22]

But if Toronto and Ottawa interests were poor-mouthing Renfrew and the calibre of hockey played in the Ottawa Valley League, others closer to the scene were not. When Renfrew journeyed to Brockville, at that city's request, to play the Montreal Wanderers in an exhibition, on January 28, 1908, a side-bet of five hundred dollars went to the winner in addition to a guarantee of four hundred dollars for travelling expenses for the teams. Renfrew defeated them handily by a 10-5 score. The Brockville newspaper reported that if the team from the small town with weekly newspapers ever situated in one of the larger cities where sporting writers could hand out the advertising as comes from Ottawa and Montreal, they would be lauded as world beaters. It continued: "Of course considerable money is behind them and it takes cash to run such an organization but every man knows his place."[23]

Even in 1908, Renfrew hockey interests knew that they must satisfy Ottawa in order to be accepted in a league with the "big boys." Renfrew supporters were reminded once again of that price when an exhibition game was arranged in February. Not only did their team lose by a score of 16-7, but it was estimated that "by doubling the score, Ottawa sports cleaned up in the neighbourhood of two thousand, five hundred dollars,"[24] from the seventy-five or so Renfrew citizens among the fifteen hundred spectators who watched the game. But that wasn't the end of their misery. Leaving Ottawa at midnight, the Grand Trunk train was side-tracked for two hours. It was bitterly cold; the trains were unheated. When it finally wheezed its way into Renfrew at 6:00 am, its bleary-eyed passengers were without heat, without money and without any love for Ottawa!

In the Ottawa Valley League, the Renfrew team flourished, continuing to build up its reputation. Having won the league championship by defeating Arnprior by a 6-3 score, the team was still in demand throughout the Valley. Yet hockey at the time was at the mercy of the elements. When Cornwall wished to erase its deficit, they arranged for an exhibition game with Renfrew, imported some players from Ottawa and heavily publicized the match. Interest was high and the residents eagerly looked forward to the contest. A great winter storm blanketed the area and the enthusiasm, keeping the size of the crowd down; when all was said and done, the deficit grew by one hundred dollars!

Even in Renfrew, where the Montreal Shamrocks were brought in for an exhibition, only four hundred attended and saw the locals win by a 7-3 score. While the crowd size was better than ten per cent of the total population, it was still disappointing. How could Renfrew hope to play in a league with Ottawa and Montreal with crowds of four hundred? To some the culprit was professionalism: the senior game was being killed off, what with these imports being brought in from outside. Renfrew did have an excellent senior team, the Rivers, but the more publicity was generated for the Creamery

Kings, the less prominent became the Rivers in the minds of the people. There were some who said that once the contests were league fixtures leading to the Stanley Cup, that would change. For this game the club had charged enormous prices; one dollar, and seventy-five cents were the reserved-seat prices, and fifty cents bought general admission.

Money was a number-one topic of conversation wherever hockey was played but especially in the Valley. Ottawa had overspent its budget of eight thousand, five hundred dollars by two hundred and fifty dollars in its losing effort to win the Stanley Cup. Followers of hockey were aghast when reports of demands from one Brandon hockey player being recruited by a Montreal club, half a continent away, included transportation for both himself and his wife to Montreal. "Next year," reported the Ottawa newspaper, "players will be wanting honeymoon tickets to Europe at the finish of the season."[25] Readers in Renfrew gasped when it was reported that Harry Smith, from Ottawa, would be paid eight hundred dollars for twelve games with the Montreal Wanderers. After all, the chief constable in Renfrew, the man who was responsible for not only maintaining the law and order but was also "sanitary inspector, truant officer, fire warden and caretaker of the fire hall,"[26] was being paid eight hundred and forty dollars - and that having been just raised from seven hundred and eighty after some debate!

The last Police Chief, Barney McDermott, had retired in 1909 and was a bit of a legend in Renfrew. Wherever there was trouble "he seemed to drop from the skies."[27] Whether the law breaker was of high rank or a drifter made no difference. Charges ranged from fast driving on the streets or over a bridge faster than a walk, not having a clean yard, selling tobacco on the Sabbath or using profane language on the street. Stories were told of the man from Calabogie, a place for which McDermott had no great love anyway, who was driving his team of horses wildly along the road. When he was stopped, obscene and blasphemous language erupted from his mouth. All of this took place on a Sunday which gave Barney McDermott even more reason to haul him before the judge. More than once he took on rowdy railroad workers celebrating noisily in one of the local pubs. Hauled before the magistrate for disturbing the peace, two were found guilty and fined three dollars or thirty days in jail.[28]

When McDermott's successor, Police Chief W.S. Banting, resigned in 1909, even though his salary had been raised the sixty dollars, it was discovered that Arnprior's police chief "earned $825. and was given an extra $25. to purchase a suit. His assistant was paid $1.75 per day, given a free suit and worked twelve hours from seven in the evening until seven the next morning."[29] In spite of that information, Renfrew chose its new police chief, Joseph Plaunt, assigned him his duties of "collector of taxes, sanitary inspector, truancy officer and general enforcer of by-laws,"[30] gave him a day from 11:00 am to 4:00 am and paid him the sum of six hundred dollars per year! Such was the value of money in the Ottawa Valley town of Renfrew in 1909.

There were two ways that Renfrew could win the Stanley Cup. One was to issue a challenge, along with every other hockey team in the country. But that would necessitate the trustees screening the many bids, and eliminating all but one or two. The combination of the Cup holders playing in a league and having a schedule and its commitments, a short playing season because of the lack of artificial ice, along with the need for the trustees to satisfy geographical considerations for the national symbol, meant that there was too long a wait involved in the challenge route. Why, in 1904, there was even a team from Dawson in the Yukon which challenged for the Cup. (They proved no contest for the Ottawa Silver Seven whose Frank McGee, a one-eyed hockey player, scored fourteen goals of the twenty-three Ottawa scored in the second of the two-game series.) Because the trustees had to be seen as fair in satisfying geographical challenges, it could be years before a club was recognized. The players could be too old even if they were held together while all these factors were being worked through.

The second way was the best. A hockey team had to be part of a league competition where the Stanley Cup was given to the pennant winner - there were no play-offs. That league in 1908 was the Eastern Canada Amateur Hockey League. When the only two amateur teams decided to withdraw from the league for the 1909 season, the decision was made to drop the word *amateur* from the title; the remaining four teams were openly professional. Thus the winner of the ECHL was awarded the Stanley Cup. That was the league that Renfrew had to get into in order to circumvent the challenge route.

Easier said than done. Ottawa and Montreal interests acted as if they had a mandate from heaven to pass the Cup between the two cities. There was little chance that upstart Renfrew would be considered for the league.

The Renfrew millionaires, however, had other ideas. M.J. O'Brien, his son Ambrose, Jim Barnet and the Liberal Member of Parliament, Tom Low, were bound and determined to bring the Stanley Cup to Renfrew. Tom Low was another self-made man who, in addition to his money and business interests in hydro power, lumber, flour mills, manufacturing and woollen mills, was also the newly elected MP for Renfrew South. Perhaps he could talk some sense into those Ottawa people!

Renfrew applied to the ECHL. Once again they were turned down. The Creamery Kings were in a quandary. They weren't able to play with Ottawa and Montreal. They just didn't seem to be able to get their attention. They weren't going to get better by playing in the Ottawa Valley League. As a matter of fact the Valley teams weren't keen on playing them either. With Renfrew's millionaire backers leading the way, the decision was made to form a new league. Overtures were made to the Senators (long a famous Ottawa name in hockey), Cornwall and Smiths Falls. Agreement was reached. Wrote the *Journal*: "The Renfrew hockey team on the principle that nothing is too good for the Irish, is now in the Federal League. Federal mind you, not provincial, district or county! Now if the Stanley Cup does not gravitate towards Renfrew about the time mothballs are beginning to bloom in the druggists' windows, it will not be because of the trustees mulishness blocking the way. It will be because of the team's ineligibility this year."[31]

The openly professional Renfrew team, known colloquially as the Federals, swept all opposition in the new league. Citizens began to take notice. Hockey, the Federals, the players and Renfrew's increased stature, perceived or otherwise, were continuing topics of conversation throughout the year. The owners brought in Bert Lindsay an outstanding goalie (and the father of later NHL star, Ted) who bought a poolroom and settled in Renfrew. Former Montreal standout Didier Pitre was signed, the Flying Frenchman, one of the outstanding players of the time. But some were not impressed. Although the town was originally settled as a community of Scots, there was a sizeable Irish contingent; what French were there seemed to keep largely to themselves. Indeed the advice was offered that the "men running the team are making an error by not having a player named Murphy on that team. . . realize they are scarce but could they not get someone to change his name?"[32]

The Irish were indeed a presence, not only in Renfrew but also in surrounding communities within a short distance such as Spruce Hedge, Springtown, Black Donald, Mount St. Patrick and Calabogie. M.J. O'Brien, Mick to those who spoke of him as if they knew him personally, was seen to be a heroic type of individual, rising as he did from the poverty of his childhood to his millionaire status. It was perhaps with a sense of the theatrical that the O'Brien Opera House, built and paid for by M.J., had its grand opening on St. Patrick's Day in 1909. Its first show was an Imperial Opera Company production called *Floradora* with tickets ranging in price from twenty-five cents to ten dollars. All of Renfrew was agog, the envy of the Valley.

Many larger cities had no such thing as an opera house. Of course, they didn't have an Irish fairy godfather like M.J. either. Could the Stanley Cup be far behind? The 1909 season would tell. If the Federals could do well in the new league, the trustees would have to accept their challenge - in spite of the Ottawa bunch. Wouldn't they?

Throughout the 1909 season, excitement mounted throughout Renfrew as the Federals demonstrated their professional talents, much to the delight of their fans and accompanied by awe throughout the Valley. All aspects of hockey were enthusiastically discussed; events not related to hockey were highlighted in hockey terms. Conversations about the huge silver finds in Cobalt, where, incidently, M.J. was deeply involved, were many, "but a certain amount of the metal refined and fashioned into a cup bearing the Stanley insignia is what people mostly think about these days."[33] Terrible puns were made about the pictures of hockey players hanging on the walls in Muir's Café, the eatery at the Argyle skating rink, home of the Federals. If anyone were to call them Muirall Decorations, it would be sufficient cause for Mr. Muir "to pull a gun and shoot with fatal effect. . . there could not be found, under the circumstances, a jury to convict him."[34]

Even the music people, in anticipation of the opening of the opera house, were framed in terms of hockey and of course the incredible sums paid to players. When, in early January, Miss Mylott, a gifted vocalist from the Antipodes, who had a singing engagement in Renfrew, reckoned her remuneration, when singing, at the rate of several dollars per minute,". . . she feels no pangs of regret over not being an expert hockeyist in a Stanley Cup country."[35]

As with many small towns, it was thought by many that Renfrew had a drinking problem but perhaps that was in the context of the town's history. In the early 1850s, it took pride in being called a temperance town, this at a time when there was open drinking at the events of the day, be they "barn raisings, logging bees, marriages, wakes. . . liquor was often dispensed along with handshakes to seal a business deal and during elections liquor was used to persuade the wavering voter to elect the right man."[36] By 1909, even with this temperance background, there were two liquor stores and eight hotels. In the first four months of the year, "some thirty odd applications (were) filled for liquor licences in the south riding of Renfrew, a circumstance which brings no joy to the clergy. Give them their way and every licence would be a marriage licence."[37] Anonymous reports were given some credence: "A minister said that a certain citizen said that Renfrew is the worst town for drinking that he has ever lived in."[38] There was still an active campaign to minimize if not eradicate the amount of consumption. In the middle of winter *The Renfrew Journal* published "Twenty cogent reasons for opposing the liquor traffic and banishing the bar":

1.　*It never builds manhood but tears it down.*

2.　*It never beautifies the home but often wrecks it.*

3.　*It never increases one's usefulness but lessens it.*

4.　*It never allays the passions but inflames them.*

5.　*It never stills the tongue of slander but loosens it.*

6.　*It never promotes purity of thought but poisons it.*

7.　*It never empties prisons and almshouses, but fills them.*

8.　*It never protects the ballot-box but defiles it.*

9.　*It never makes happy families but miserable ones.*

10.　*It never prompts to right doing in anything but to wrong.*

11.　*It never prepares one for heaven but for hell.*

12.　*It never diminishes taxes (with all its revenue) but increases them.*

13.　*It never renders the Sabbath quiet but desecrates it.*

14.　*It never protects our property nor personal safety but endangers them.*

15. *It never helps to get a good insurance policy on life but militates against it.*

16. *It never creates ambition and thrift, but crime.*

17. *It never builds up the church but peoples the station house, prisons and chain gangs.*

18. *It never refines character nor promotes Christian grace but is a destroyer of the soul.*

19. *It never teaches honesty and uprightness but invites the incendiary to apply the midnight torch.*

20. *It never promotes the man but robs him of his money, his family happiness, his good home, his hope and all endearments of life.*[39]

Will Lee, in his column *Here and There*, could not resist not-so-subtle digs at the temperance advocates and indeed at whomever seemed to take themselves too seriously. When the Brockville Invincibles lost convincingly to Renfrew ("If the Invincibles, here last night don't change their name, they are humourists, not hockeyists"), it was noted "that there were hundreds at the hockey match on the evening of January 14, whereas there were only scores at the lecture in the Temperance Hall the same evening. An explanation is easy. Consumption we have with us always whereas hockey is good only three months of the twelve!"[40]

Naturally, in an agricultural community, there was a constant interest in the price of grains and livestock. Even these were sometimes related to the hockey situation, as if to underscore the dictum that you can explain anything to people if you can put it into terms that they can understand. When a news story from Brockville highlighted the sale of a "couple of cows," it was for "a figure exceeding even the salary of professional hockey players."[41]

The skating rink and the hockey team were becoming the number-one topic of conversation. Renfrew's continued winning ways sat well with all. But that didn't mean that fun couldn't be poked at this sacred cow. Games which were advertised to begin at 8:15 pm were described as "pleasant fiction."[42] The covered, natural-ice surface depended upon the cold weather but at the same time, the spectators were likely to freeze their feet unless there was some action to keep them moving and preoccupied. When a game was late in starting, as they invariably were, reports commented on the bitter cold and "some impatience waiting for the fun to commence after the advertised hour had passed."[43]

Hockey and the Federals were the centre of Renfrew's universe. Followers of the team often waited after the game at Muir's to catch a glimpse of their heroes at the Rink Café where team players and officials gathered to be fêted by Mr. Muir's catering service. When in Ottawa, a city much larger than Renfrew, and of course the national capital, many events were being held simultaneously with hockey, there was no doubt as to their relative importance. Tongue firmly imbedded in his cheek, Lee commented that "in Ottawa, a hockey match and events of minor importance took place e.g. opening of Parliament, a stock show and horse races. If Parliament will open and other events occur just as a hockey match is on with all the world watching, they have only themselves to blame if ranking merely as 'and others'."[44]

Three of the stalwart players in Renfrew's 1909 line-up were Bert Lindsay, Didier Pitre and another Montrealer, Ernie Liffiton. Pitre, known as Cannonball because of his hard shot, was born in Sault Ste. Marie, had played with Montreal, Portage and the Shamrocks before he showed up in Renfrew. Wags were likely to write of such an itinerant player that he "frequently changes his post-office address." [45]

As a result, because of what were appearing to be frequent deviations from the traditional approaches to sporting practices, there were periodic reminders of the role and place of sport as well as its heritage and roots:

*Play Fair: This principle must be made dominant in our Canadian life. It must rule in the school yards. Our boys must* be *taught to regard the unfair as the contemptible. We must call them to cherish and develop the spirit of fair play that should be our heritage as a child of the British Empire. It should rule in our sports as it does in those of the motherland. The player who takes a mean disadvantage should be hissed off the field. Unfairness should be classed as horse drugging, dice loading and card marking.*[46]

It wasn't the only reminder that some felt that the good citizens of Renfrew needed. Located in the midst of a farming and lumbering community, there were some deep-rooted patterns of behaviour that were hard to reshape. Yet it was obvious that the times were beginning to change. The telephone and the automobile were making their way into daily life, although not all were ready to accept the new reality. There was the German farmer out of town towards Eganville who was unhappy with the trains which frightened his livestock. He built a fence across the tracks, much to the consternation of railroad officials. The CPR supplied a special train to take the Renfrew constable to the site. Joined by the engineer and baggage man, the officer explained the situation to the farmer who was in the middle of his chores. Having finished them, the farmer led the group to the farmhouse where he had an animated discussion, in German, with his wife about the situation. The farmer climbed up a ladder to the loft, to change his clothes it was assumed. After a few minutes, he called down to his wife who in turn climbed up the ladder. A few more minutes passed by. Again, the farmer called downstairs; his daughter moved up the ladder in response. The other daughter followed suit. After half an hour, the Renfrew constable called upstairs for the farmer. He wasn't coming down! The constable went up. The farmer swung a club to knock him back down. Before the skirmish was over and the farmer brought back downstairs, the man's wife, two daughters and dog all had to be fought off. It was an exhausted constable and helpers who returned to the creamery town, their prisoner in chains,[47] the railroad line open once again, perhaps much to the chagrin of other farmers who were dismayed at the iron horse, hissing, spitting, puffing and clattering through the fields, upsetting the peace and tranquillity and perhaps the production of the dairy herd and poultry.

But this was the twentieth century, the new era. Times were changing and citizens were encouraged to change their old ways, to move with the times. Indeed, every time they saw Jim Barnet travelling down Renfrew's dirt roads, scaring all the horses and causing all heads to turn as his beautiful new 1907 Oldsmobile, a horseless carriage some had called it, moved ever so magically through town, it was a visible reminder that a new age had dawned. When Barnet's first car had arrived in 1907 by Grand Trunk Railroad, there was a great stir in town. His second roadster, another Oldsmobile, arrived the same way and was followed by a succession: townsfolk buying Russels, Mitchells, Reos, a Peerless and M.J. O'Brien with his Pierce Arrow.[48]

When Mayor Arthur Gravelle was elected to that position in 1909, his inaugural address on January 11 highlighted yet another custom to be sublimated. The mayor launched an offensive against spitting! Everybody spat! It was like a civic pastime! Why, there were spittoons in the bars, hotel lobbies and public buildings! Spitting was almost a national rite! As far as Mayor Gravelle was concerned though, it was time to change that. There was to be no spitting on sidewalks and floors, especially those of public buildings. Spitting wasn't to be banned, it was carefully pointed out, it was to be directed, for matters of decency and public health. Gravelle did feel that it should be banned but that wasn't what was being advocated: "It is just as easy to spit into the gutters as on the walks when on the street and no inconvenience to the practised expectorator to hit a spittoon when within doors."[49]

There might have been a damper put on expectorations but none such cap on Renfrew's hockey expectations. It wasn't so much that the fans wanted to see the Brockville Invincibles when they arrived for the January 8 contest, it was more that the eight hundred fans went "to size up the local septet more than to see a well contested contest."[50] When all of Renfrew's teams had won in the week prior, the *Journal* trumpeted:

*Renfrew's great week in hockey - four wins and no losses.*

*Renfrew Pros 24 Cornwall 12*

*Rivers 12 Pembroke 2*

*Collegiate 5 Pembroke High School 2*

*Pros 9 Ottawa Senators 2* [51]

Regarding the 24-12 score, the *Journal* crowed: "It wasn't a winter form of cricket or curling, it was hockey, at least such was the announcement on the posters and posters never joke."[52]

Each new week in the winter of '09 was greeted with another Renfrew victory: Renfrew, 23, Smiths Falls, 2; Renfrew,7, Cornwall, 3; Renfrew, 18, Smiths Falls, 4; Renfrew,12, Ottawa Senators, 2. They were a joy to behold. The players seemed to mesh beautifully, all seven men seemingly knowing where everyone was and would be. To many, it didn't appear that there was any finer expression anywhere .

It was seven-man hockey played in two thirty-minute halves. Each goal that was scored was considered a game. The competitions, therefore, were described as contests or matches or meetings but never games as they are today. A face-off followed each goal and whichever team won the most games, i.e. scored the most goals, in sixty minutes, won. There were no substitutions allowed. If a player was injured and could not continue, the opponents also removed a player from the ice. Team-mates were to be always behind the puck when a member of their team was carrying it; they had to shinny on their own side. The goal-tender was unable to leave his feet at any time in order to stop the puck. And of course there were no masks, but that didn't stop some players from lifting the puck up around the goalie's head - by mistake of course.

Equipment was somewhat flimsy; stiff paper or magazines could be used to buttress what passed for shin-pads. A goalie might be seen to wear cricket pads. Players were constantly borrowing ideas from other sports. Baseball caps were in vogue if a game was played outdoors; when facing the sun, the peak was forward, going away, it was turned to the back. Percy LeSueur, the great Ottawa net-minder in 1909, was the first to use a baseball trapper mitt, with added padding inserted, to catch the puck.

The terms *point* and *cover-point* were still in vogue although some were beginning to use the term *defence* for the pair. It was probably the Toronto Argonauts 1906 team play which led to the use of the term defence. They lined up beside each other in a play-off game with Berlin and, being successful, were copied by other teams. The change was made in terminology as well to left and right defence.[53] But away from the Ontario League, at the face-off, the point would stand about fifteen feet in front of the goalie, the cover-point another fifteen feet in front of him. Most of the teams used larger immobile points and cover-points who would try to slow down the opponents with body-checks and if they handled the puck at all, lifted it (raised it) far down the ice to relieve pressure. The Federals changed that with their new style. Their points played more like forwards, rushing up the ice, getting involved in the play, passing it to a team-mate, looking for the return pass and generally assuming a more offensive role. "Body-checking is going out and nobody bemoans it,"[54] reported one wag, perhaps somewhat wishfully.

The centre and left and right-wings made up the forward line and were likely to be more involved in the play. It was the rover, the seventh man, who was a hybrid of all positions. He was the key man, usually the best skater with good balance ready to shift himself to wherever needed. He could follow his attacking team-mate looking for a rebound or a drop-pass. Defensively, he came back on every play, frequently pestering the puck carrier, sometimes steering him into an unseen body-check! All made for a tremendously entertaining, gripping match that was more than just a game; it gave some soul to winter, it made it come alive!

And when the season was over? Well, "somebody has said that a skating rink in the summer season looks as lonely as an old maid at a wedding."[55] That was so particularly in the summer of '09. The *Journal 's* front page said it best as it boasted of Renfrew's successes in hockey and curling and its quest for the future:

*What We Have We Hold*
*The Central Canada Curling Association Tankard*
*The Low Challenge Cup (Curling) County*
*The Citizen Shield Hockey Championship*
*The Federal Hockey Championship*
*What we have not, we'll reach for - The Stanley Cup!*[56]

Renfrew's reach would have to extend to Ottawa where the Stanley Cup was on prominent display in the windows of Messrs Rosenthal and Sons jewellery store, "swathed in streamers of red, white and black,"[57] the colours of the Ottawa team. Trustee William Foran had publicly stated that Renfrew and Winnipeg would be allowed to challenge for the trophy during the next season.

*Frank Cosentino*

34

FRANK PATRICK OF RENFREW CLUB

# *Chapter Two*

## *The NHA — Beginnings*

It was a sorrowful Renfrew group that heard the news that its bid for a Stanley Cup challenge was turned down, contrary to Mr. Foran's announcement. Sure, they weren't alone; Cobalt and Edmonton were also denied but not Winnipeg and Galt. It became even more important for the Creamery Kings to leave the Federal and enter the big league.

To that end, a delegation headed to Montreal for the annual meeting of the Eastern Canada Hockey Association, a group not without its own problems. Their owners wanted to put the professional game on a better business basis, using baseball as its model. There was a move afoot to draft rules for the buying and selling and trading of players. Largely at the instigation of Ottawa, owners felt that since they were paying the salaries, they should have more control and that those salaries should be more regulated. Some even felt that a limit should be placed on the salaries, a move which was sure to cause strong protest from the players.

It was all tied to the same problem. Players flitted from one team to another, wherever the money was better, getting the best deal for themselves. Sure, the teams were vying with each other to win the Stanley Cup, but this was an association, the argument went, they were all in this together. There had to be a set of rules and regulations which would allow the competition to remain entirely on the ice.

And there were other problems. The league needed a better balance of games. On a home-and-home basis, four teams would only provide six games for the season. More were needed. Yet the previous year's double schedule of six home and six away was too much. The logical answer would have been to have nine games but no club was willing to lose its advantage, not to say greater gate receipts, by having more away than home games. The short season was dictated by the vagaries of the weather, the travel conditions, the train schedules and, of course, by the weekends, since most of the players also held down full-time jobs.

Ideally, all seemed to agree, a single schedule, home-and-home, was needed, but with six teams, providing a ten-game season.

But which six teams? Certainly, Ottawa would be one. In fact they appeared to have too much power. It seemed that they were dictating to everybody, but then, power seemed to follow naturally the team which held the Stanley Cup. Indeed, legends were beginning to be believed about the divine right of the famed Silver Seven or the Senators but better known to everyone in the game as the Ottawas. On the surface, it appeared relatively straightforward. There were four teams presently in the Association: Ottawa, Quebec, the Shamrocks (Montreal) and the Wanderers (Montreal). Two others were to be found and the ideal would be reached.

It soon became obvious that there was much going on behind the scenes. During the previous season, the executive of the Wanderers had resigned, handing the club over to a new group but with the stipulation that the club not be sold. The new executive disregarded the directive and what's more, made a commitment to play its games in the newer but smaller Jubilee rink rather than the larger Wood Avenue arena. The new franchise associates were P.J. Doran, owner of the Jubilee, James Strachan, a Montreal baker, R.R. "Dickie" Boon and

James "Jimmy" Gardner. The move made great sense to this group since they also owned the rink and would be able to maximize the gate receipts, but the rest of the Association members were upset since their forty-per-cent cut would be smaller at the new facility. They could argue that they had a loyalty to former owner William Jennings but, coincidently, he owned the larger arena!

Prior to the scheduled meeting of November 13, 1909, at the Windsor Hotel in Montreal, William Jennings, former president of the Wanderers, trained to Ottawa to meet their club officials. It was November 11. Ottawa officials Llewellyn Bate and Dave Mulligan discussed the situation with Jennings for hours at the Russell House. It reminded some of the traditional Ottawa/Wanderer compact, where, bound by common interests, the two clubs shaped the Association in their preferred image.That agreement was supposed to have lapsed. Yet it was obvious that Ottawa was still the kingmaker; the former executive of the Wanderers was acknowledging that. Jennings informed Bate and Mulligan that the Wanderer franchise had been sold to Mr. Doran without the approval of those who had authority. Doran, thinking that he had purchased the franchise in good faith for seven hundred and fifty dollars, was reported to have spent some three thousand, two hundred dollars to keep the players together at the end of the 1908/09 season. According to Jennings, while Doran currently held the Wanderer franchise, he had obtained it from a person who had acted on his own behalf. He had no such authority to do so.

When the meeting broke up, an agreement was made that Ottawa would stand by Jennings; that the Ottawa club would deny membership to the Jubilee-rink group; that the Ottawa/Wanderer compact was back on the rails. And Renfrew? There was hope!

But not for long - on all counts! At an informal meeting on November 13, prior to the three o'clock official beginning, a derailment of sorts took place. Having gotten wind of the

November 11 meeting, the new Wanderer-franchise owners requested an "audience" with Ottawa to present their side of the story. They privately produced documents addressed "to whom it may concern," that, "William Jennings, President, Thomas G. Hodge, Vice-President, George G. Gates, secretary and R.R. Boon, member of the Executive, of the Wanderers Hockey Club had transferred to Fred C. Strachan, personally, all their interests in the Wanderer Hockey Club."[1] Further, Mr. Strachan was to cover all debts incurred by the club as well as receive all moneys accruing to the club.

Now the Ottawas were thoroughly confused. After all, there was such a thing as honour involved. If the club had been sold without authorization, that was one thing, but now it seemed that Fred Strachan and his agent, P.J. Doran, were the legal owners of the Wanderers. . . and they wanted to play at the smaller Jubilee rink!

There was more. When the three o'clock meeting convened, the Association president, Joe Power, was absent, sick with pneumonia. The Chair was to be filled by the Vice-President, Fred Strachan, not exactly an impartial observer. This was too much for the other three clubs. Citing a need to consult with their respective memberships, a motion for adjournment was made and passed. The continuation of the meeting was to occur November 25, at the Windsor Hotel in Montreal.

The old Wanderers wasted no time in seizing the initiative. On November 16, Art Ross was named as player-manager. The former member of the 1907 Kenora (Rat Portage) and 1908 Montreal Wanderers Stanley Cup teams, and who was later to lend his name to the trophy awarded to the NHL's leading scorer, was already a widely known hockeyist. Having its headquarters in the Wood Avenue arena, the club, known as the All Montreal, was hoping to attract its former followers and cash in on the rivalry already developing with the upstart Jubilee-rink offshoots. They quickly announced that Riley, Hern and Smaill, all members of the Stanley Cuppers, would return with Ross.

Meanwhile, it was an open-minded Ambrose O'Brien who made his way from Renfrew to Montreal, arriving on November 24th. Not only was he interested in the ECHA meeting on the 25th, but trustees Ross and Foran were to announce the names of the teams who would challenge Ottawa for the Cup. Earlier in the year, Renfrew had been mentioned as a distinct probability but with Ottawa's meddling, who could tell? The announcement was to be made on the 24th. There was an impressive list of possibilities: Galt, winner of the Ontario Professional League, Winnipeg, champions of Manitoba, Renfrew, conquerors of the Federal, Cobalt, champions of Témiscaming, and Edmonton, the Alberta victors. O'Brien felt confident. In addition to Bert Lindsay and the rest of the Federal League champions, he had first call on Didier Pitre, the outstanding French Canadian who had been part of Edmonton's unsuccessful challenge the previous year. Yes, the twenty-four-year-old was confident that he had the nucleus to defeat the Ottawa club. . . and win the Stanley Cup.

But, would he ever get the chance? Not yet! When the trustees made their announcement, Renfrew was virtually ignored. Galt and Winnipeg were successful. Edmonton was next in line - if time was available, or one of the teams selected not able to show. Cobalt and Renfrew were out in the cold - again.

But there was still one chance. Renfrew had applied to the Eastern Canada Hockey Association whose adjourned meeting was due to reconvene the next day. O'Brien set about lobbying the various clubs. The Montreal Shamrocks, a group representing Montreal's Irish Canadians was first. Surely they would be receptive to an O'Brien. Their owner, Harry McLaughlin, was sympathetic. He assured Ambrose of their support. Now there was life. O'Brien approached Fred Strachan of the Wanderers in his tenuous role. Again, an indication of support. Yet both teams hedged. They wanted to see what Ottawa's reaction would be.

"Ottawa, again," O'Brien was heard to mutter under his breath.

Waiting in the lobby of the Windsor Hotel, Ambrose O'Brien was determined to speak to the Ottawa delegates, Dave Mulligan and Percy Butler, prior to their entering the meeting room. It was just before the dinner hour; both Ottawa men were on their way into the dining-room. O'Brien intercepted them, asking them for a few moments of their time. Well, yes, but they didn't have very long, they said.

When O'Brien said that he wanted a franchise for Renfrew, the two Ottawa men could hardly contain their smirks. O'Brien persisted, reviewing all the hockey successes of the creamery town. Trying to disguise the tone of condescension, the two said that they would certainly keep Renfrew in mind and off they went into the dining-room, looking straight ahead all the while. O'Brien went back to the lobby, seething inside at the smug, patronizing attitude of the men and the club which seemed to control who would and who would not challenge for the Stanley Cup.

When the adjourned meeting reconvened that evening, it was obvious that there had been much consultation in the intervening time. What started off as a routine session soon developed into anything but.The application of the Nationals and those of Cornwall and Renfrew were read into the record. Almost immediately Dave Mulligan declared that the ECHL, as it existed, would be somewhat limited in its scope and then "put a torch to the gunpowder by tendering the resignation of Ottawa from the ECHL." Mulligan continued by advocating reorganization; Ottawa's resignation should be considered the first step towards that goal. The Shamrocks, Quebec and the Wanderers were left to carry on; President Lundy declared that it was impossible to do that with three clubs. As if by a prearranged signal, the Shamrocks' delegate J. O'Brien, no relation to Ambrose, tendered that club's withdrawal. The two remaining clubs followed suit. When Mr. Lundy, in the Chair, suggested an adjournment of the meeting, it hardly seemed necessary "since every delegate in the room had practically withdrawn."[2]

The Ottawa, Shamrocks and Quebec representatives gathered together for some last-minute consultations, their sixth such deliberation since the first adjournment. The Wanderers were left to mingle with all the other clubs which had come to the meeting seeking entry. The "big three" attempted to lay the groundwork for a new league, informally discussing the relative merits of the other applicants. Now included were the Wanderers along with All Montreal (a group of former Wanderers who, importantly, would play their games in the Wood Avenue arena), the Nationals (a group representing the French element of Montreal who would also play at Wood Avenue), Cornwall, and Renfrew.

After some time, the meeting was opened "to all those interested in hockey." All the delegates filed into the room, somewhat bewildered by the events as they were unfolding. Lundy, again, was in the Chair, by mutual consent of the three in control. More likely it was because of Ottawa's approval and the others' acquiescence. Applications to the "ECHL or Senior hockey or whatever they chose to call it," were invited. The five responded and were asked to withdraw from the meeting. After some discussion the French Canadian team, the Nationals, was accepted on the understanding that they "played at the Arena and had no vote until the League was complete."

*Then the naughty point of the whole meeting turned up, Wanderers for All Montreal. That sore point, a selling of the Wanderers franchise, still apparently aches. Messrs. Jennings and Hodge were first admitted and explained their side of the story, stating that although it was not written in black and white, it was an understood thing that the Wanderer franchise was not to be sold when the club was turned over to the present management. Following the explanation, Fred Strachan was admitted to say his little piece. Freddy also told that the Wanderers would play in the Arena if wanted. There followed more consultations on the part of Ottawa, Shamrocks and Quebec with the National representatives taking no part in the discussion. Finally, just as the early hours of the morning were approaching, All Montreal was declared admitted.*[3]

The admission stopped at five clubs; approval in principle was given to a double schedule. Lundy was again elected President, Sparks of Ottawa, Vice-President, and Emmett Quinn of Montreal, the Secretary. The remaining member of the Executive was W.J. Lynch of Quebec. Thirty-five dollars was asked from each member as an initiation fee; twenty-five dollars was set as the annual dues. The new league also agreed to take over the debts of the ECHL, some sixty dollars. The next meeting was to be held on December 4, at which time a schedule and constitution were to be adopted. It all seemed matter of fact. The deed was done. Things were proceeding as smoothly as they should.

It was obvious that Ottawa, as Stanley Cup holders, controlled the meeting, that the large arena facilities and its ability to generate gate receipts was paramount. Gone were the Wanderers. In their stead were the All Montreals, a collection of former Wanderers under the guidance of Art Ross and Jennings and Hodge from the old gang. The compact was back in business.

With the acceptance of the Nationals, the league would have representatives in Montreal from the French, Irish and English communities. The prize for the double schedule of sixteen games was to be the Stanley Cup. The whole thing smacked of an earlier time when, in 1905, Ottawa and the Wanderers had abandoned the Federal League and joined with the Shamrocks and Quebec, who had left the Canadian Amateur Hockey League.

All the details were unknown, of course, to those who were excluded from the discussions. Delegates were in various areas of the hotel waiting for news of their applications. Ambrose O'Brien sat, rather impatiently, in the lobby as the night unfolded and turned into morning. He was unaware that the Wanderers were being frozen out of the new league. Lucky, too. If he had known, he probably would have been devastated. After all, he was counting on their support to sway the others! At the very least, he would have liked to have been able to address the group personally. Not that he distrusted Jimmy Gardner of the Wanderers; he just preferred to do his own talking on his own behalf.

When Gardner came storming out of the meeting "swearing like a trooper,"[4] he headed directly for O'Brien. The Renfrew man was momentarily startled. Was Gardner that much behind the Valley town's bid? The situation looked grim. When Gardner explained all, everything became clear. The two of them sat on the couch in the lobby, each one looking as if he had lost his last and best friend. Then the Montrealer turned to O'Brien, an inquisitive look in his eyes. Did the O'Briens still have an interest in teams up north, in Cobalt and Haileybury, he asked. Yes, nodded Ambrose. Now Gardner became animated, enthusiastic:

*Ambrose, why don't you and I form a league? You've got Cobalt and Haileybury and Renfrew. We have the Wanderers. And, I think that if a team of all Frenchmen was formed in Montreal, it would be a real draw. We could give it a French Canadian name. . .* [5]

This might have been somewhat apocryphal. The Toronto *Globe* reported, "the Renfrew hockey Club had another card up its sleeve. Not satisfied that they are frozen out of the big league, they are moving in the direction of a mammoth new league. Cobalt, Haileybury, Wanderers and Montreal Nationals and Cornwall have been invited to enter, the intention being to run a league in opposition to the new Canadian Hockey League."[6]

When O'Brien returned to Renfrew, there was a note of excitement in his voice as he recounted the details of his conversation with Gardner. Rumours were rampant that Cornwall, then Toronto, would join the new league. . . . calls were put out to Haileybury and Cobalt. George Martel, M.J., Ambrose and Barnet all began busying themselves, branching out, contacting prospects. Rumours. . . . sure enough, the hockey season was back and everyone had a favoured insight into what was going on. But always, at least in Renfrew, there was one universally held opinion: Renfrew had been knifed in the back to stop them being selected to play for the Stanley Cup and Ottawa was to blame! They would have to be made to pay for their uppitiness.

One of the first actions taken by the Renfrew group was to see if another group of Ottawa people wanted to enter the proposed league. Harvey Pulford and Alf Smith were contacted. The former stars of the Senators were willing but all the best dates in the arena had been taken by the Stanley Cup team. No other suitable facility was available. It was bad news. The new league needed all the large arenas it could get if it was going to survive in the smaller towns. Travel and salaries would otherwise be too much of a burden.

Meanwhile, the Stanley Cup champions did not stand still. Amid more rumours that Renfrew would make a grab for its players in order to put its team together, a concerted effort was made to secure them for the upcoming season. Goalie Perc LeSueur agreed to play goal for one thousand dollars; Bruce Ridpath and Lester Patrick were being sought to bolster the champions. The players were ready to take advantage of the new competitive situation; record salaries were being demanded by all. Ottawa, however, was said "to surely have a diamond-studded team, no matter how high they go for them."[7]

*They* referred to Renfrew, of course. Everybody was fast becoming aware of that. But as far as Renfrew was concerned high indeed was where they were prepared to go.

On December 2, 1909, the four clubs, the Wanderers, Renfrew, Cobalt and Haileybury met to form a new league at 200 St. James Street in Montreal, the offices of Dominion Office And Store Fitting Company, Limited, situated in the St. Lawrence Hall Hotel.[8] The Wanderers were represented by Strachan, Gardner, Doran and Boon; Renfrew by Ambrose O'Brien, George Martel, and Jim Barnet; Tommy Hare and Noah Timmins were there from Cobalt and Haileybury, respectively.

*The Gazette* wasn't impressed by the challenge, calling it, "in its tentative state, easily the most pretentious organization that has yet been attempted by hockey clubs in Canada."

Regardless, the proposed-league officials sat down to discuss operations and strategy. Some of it already seemed to be obvious. They needed players to attract the public from the Canadian Association, and to win the Stanley Cup - not necessarily in that order - and money was to be no object.

There was lots of money; it would be spent freely and be guided by "business principles as applied to baseball."[9] Clubs, upon leaving home, would play more than one game in an attempt to minimize travel expenses. In order to solidify their new partnership, three clubs posted a one thousand dollar bond that Thursday night. The fourth did so on Friday morning. It was not only a token of good faith, it reinforced the commitment that the franchise would not be sold for at least one year. Even then, a two-third vote of the league would be necessary. These men were serious. Each point was hammered out so that there was no lack of understanding as to where they all stood. Always, the motive of undermining the rival league acted as the standard: the name for the group was chosen - The National Hockey Association. With an increased amount of satisfaction, the meeting was adjourned to December 4.

To an impartial observer, it might have appeared that when Ottawa interests were not impressed with the new league, regarding it "as a bluff,"[10] Renfrew seemed to turn up the heat. In what was described as the "biggest offer ever made,"[11] George Martel had tried to entice Fred Taylor, the Listowel Cyclone, to leave Ottawa for Renfrew. The capital was in a flap. Taylor, a cover-point, was thought by many to be the best player in the game, the Bobby Orr, Wayne Gretzky, and Mario Lemieux of the day all rolled into one. He had been offered the unheard-of salary of two thousand dollars, plus a job paying more than twelve hundred dollars to captain and manage the Renfrew team! The Ottawas might have been in disarray at the news, but in Montreal, at the National Hockey Association meetings, there was uproarious laughter as all imagined the sputtering reactions of the Ottawa executive.

Whether by design or coincidence, the offer, which had been made some days previously, had only been publicized December 3 in an exclusive story by the Ottawa *Citizen*. Some saw the fine hand of the O'Briens behind the exclusive. In any event, the new league was the recipient of reams of publicity it could never hope to buy.

Immediately, the Ottawa club's player committee gathered. Taylor was summoned. There was a sense of urgency. After all, here was the possibility of losing their best player. What with the upcoming Stanley Cup challenges and this upstart league vying for public support, they simply could not afford it. It would give legitimacy to the National League. At 5:00 pm, Friday, December 3, Taylor met with Messrs Bates and Mulligan at the Russell House. It was a reassuring meeting. Ottawa surely did not want to lose Taylor; they would do all in their power to satisfy his wishes. Taylor, for his part, didn't want to cause any problems. He was simply trying to better himself both off and on the ice. It was settled, then. Taylor would stay with Ottawa. No contracts were signed; Ottawa, in the spirit of the old school, didn't believe in them. A person's word was his bond. Taylor's word was given in return for a "price almost equal to that which Renfrew offered Taylor."[12] The news spread like wildfire in the capital. The gloom which had hit it was dispelled. Taylor's words had a soothing effect: "I have just written to Renfrew telling them that I am going to stay in Ottawa. They offered me two thousand and a position alright but I'm now going to continue with Ottawa. Negotiations with Renfrew are off as far as I'm concerned."[13]

But not as far as Renfrew was. It wasn't the first time that they had tried to entice Taylor from Ottawa. They almost succeeded in the 1907/08 season, Taylor's first year with Ottawa. The *Free Press* had broken the story then on the eve of Ottawa's first game of the season. Concerned that Taylor had not appeared for the practice prior to the game, they had it on reliable authority that the new player had taken the train to Renfrew. Quickly, the Ottawa secretary, John Dickson, was dispatched to find him. There was a suspicion that M.J. O'Brien had had something to do with this. On his entry into the Upper Ottawa Valley League, he had publicly stated that Renfrew was going to pursue the Stanley Cup, vigorously! Stopping first at the Dominion Hotel, and establishing that Taylor had indeed checked in there but had left in the company of a gentleman with a coonskin coat and bowler hat, Dickson took off down the main street. Before long, he had spotted the two. Allowing them to finish their conversation and witnessing the two shake hands upon parting, Dickson moved in. After moving into a private suite at the hotel, Dickson was told that Taylor was under the impression that Ottawa really didn't want him, that they had enough players without him to recapture the Cup. When he was assured that he had been listening to the wrong people, Taylor, much to the chagrin of the Renfrew delegation, who appeared a few minutes later in the hope of translating the handshake into a contract signature, decided to remain with Ottawa:

*"Gentlemen, now that I fully understand the situation, I wouldn't play here for the whole darn town, with this hotel thrown in". He nodded politely to the open-mouthed Renfrew delegation, smiled agreeably at Mr. Dickson and the two of them left the room together. They had dinner, a pleasant walk around town and then caught the train back to Ottawa.*[14]

Renfrew's ambition to harness the power of the Cyclone would continue. Indeed Renfrew and the upstart league were like a gale force. Renfrew made offers to every member of the 1909/10 Ottawa team, including Marty Walsh and Albert Kerr. Tommy Hare of Cobalt was said to have been making "reckless bids"[15]; lamented *The Globe:*

*The buck chasers are reaping a bountiful harvest as a result of the war between the rival leagues. Many believe that the formation of the Association has brought about the crisis in hockey and that*

*the frenzied financing for men will result disastrously for the clubs
and the game. Money talks now. There is no sentiment.*

Whether by design or coincidence, the National Hockey
Association reconvened at a meeting on Saturday, December
4, in Montreal's Windsor Hotel. It seemed to be saying, in
every way possible, that it was going to challenge the Canadian
League's turf in every way. The Windsor Hotel had been a
popular meeting place for sport organizations for years. The
linking of the new organization with this hotel's name seemed
to give the impression of quality and tradition. The National
Association gathered in room one hundred and twenty-nine,
just down the corridor from one hundred and thirty-five where
the CHL was also in session. Reporters had a field-day,
positioning themselves where they could see if there was any
movement from one room to the other. There were reports
that Ottawa and the Montreal Nationals wanted to join the
new league: Ottawa with the hope that the raiding of its
players would stop and it could resume the old compact with
the Wanderers; The Nationals, the Canadian League's version
of a team of French Canadians, were having problems with
rinks and seemed to be leaning to the Jubilee rink, with its
better terms and dates. There was other gossip too. Overtures
were supposed to have been made to Renfrew and the
Wanderers to join the Canadian Hockey League. The loss of
the two strongest supporters of the National would certainly
weaken the upstart group. But it was too late. Two weeks ago,
there was a good chance that an offer might have been
accepted but now, it looked as if the old league was on the run
from the new enterprise. . . and there was the bond to consider.

The fifth NHA team was accepted at that December 4
meeting when Les Canadiens came into being. Tommy Hare of
Cobalt, acting as an agent of the O'Briens, "put up the security
for the Club and a guarantee of fifteen (sic) thousand dollars
cash for the players' salaries."[16] The plan called for the team
ownership to be transferred as soon as possible "to a number
of French Canadian sportsmen."[17] Jack Laviolette "probably

the most famous French Canadian player of the game,"[18] was named manager. The team lost no time in courting the public. It announced its first major acquisition almost immediately: Didier Pitre would play for the Canadiens. The announcement was somewhat premature. Pitre was also being actively pursued by the Nationals. In fact, it said that it had Pitre signed and would go to court if necessary to prove it. Not far behind in announcements was the name of Newsy Lalonde. The Canadiens also dropped his name, saying that the great scorer would also be joining them from the Toronto team in the Ontario Professional League. The commitment was also made that the Canadiens would have first chance at signing any French Canadian available in order to have them as the focus of French communities everywhere.

One other franchise was also awarded. Toronto would come into the Association but not until 1911 or 1912.

While both groups were wary of releasing any information which might be considered helpful to the others, including for example their respective schedules, the NHA announced its executive: M. Doheny of Renfrew was elected President; Thomas Hare, Cobalt, Vice-President; Secretary-Treasurer, John McCafferty, Toronto.

Named to the Executive were: M.J. O'Brien, Renfrew; Slate, Haileybury; Boon, Wanderers; Laviolette, Canadiens and Hare of Cobalt. The Association also announced that it would use a standard contract for its players and that professional referees would be used. The NHA also showed some shrewdness. Rather than spend a lot of money, time and effort creating a new constitution and by-laws, it simply adopted that of the Eastern Canada Hockey Association, since no one was using it anyway. They had gone out of business a few days earlier. Sunday games were also discussed but there were a number of objections, particularly by the Wanderers; it was simply too controversial a move. The idea was dropped.

The NHA was fully aware that it would be an uphill battle against the Canadian League and its Stanley Cup-champion member, Ottawa. After all, its population centres were much smaller. It could only survive by bonding together,by being a true association with all teams contributing. Thus, when informal feelers from two other clubs, including Ottawa, were put out at the meeting, the Wanderers' Gardner was adamant. He, for one, was having nothing to do with an unprincipled group of people who were ready to cast you aside at a moment's notice. It was obvious that he was quite heated at the prospect. Ambrose O'Brien made light of the situation: if Gardner wanted the League to fold, leaving all of Montreal for the NHA, the surest way would be to take some of the teams in and exclude the others.[19]

FRED. TAYLOR of Renfrew Club.

# Chapter Three

## Taylor Made

With the meeting of the National Hockey Association over,
the clubs, and particularly Renfrew, set about gathering
players for the 1910 season. Ottawa, with its Stanley Cup cast,
was a prime target. Renfrew offered Albert Kerr and Marty
Walsh two thousand, three hundred dollars plus a job at twelve
hundred dollars! To underline the seriousness of the bid, M.J.
himself met with the players in Ottawa's Windsor Hotel,
personally guaranteeing that the money would be deposited to
their credit at a bank of their choosing, in Ottawa, Renfrew,
Kingston or Brockville! And not only that, he was willing to
guarantee the contracts for two years![1] George Martel was
also busy. Two other Ottawa players were approached by him:
Fred Lake and, once again, Fred Taylor. Each was offered
three thousand dollars for the season, with a
twelve-hundred-dollar paying position in Renfrew thrown in to
sweeten the deal. The money would be deposited in the
Merchants' Bank in Renfrew in their names. [2]

The news created a whirlwind of controversy. All of the
players were acknowledged stars but could any player be
worth that much for playing a game? One Toronto newspaper
cattishly queried: "let us see. What salary does the average
teacher in Renfrew get?"[3]

While they were certainly supportive of education, the millionaire backers of the creamery-town hockey club, M.J. O'Brien, Ambrose O'Brien, James Barnet and Thomas Low, MP, were more concerned at the moment with icing a team to capture the Stanley Cup. And if Ottawa's Stanley Cup team was decimated in the process, so much the better. It appeared that they were going to get their wish too. All interested parties had gathered in an Ottawa sporting-goods store, all set to sign contracts with Renfrew. Never in their wildest dreams had the players thought that they could earn so much from hockey and now, even though they had to leave Ottawa to do so, it was about to happen. The Renfrew delegation was thrilled too. With these four as their nucleus, the Stanley Cup was as good as theirs.

It was too good to be true. Ottawa executive members burst into the store. They wanted to speak with the players. Rumours later circulated that they had been informed by Fred Taylor as to what was happening, where it was happening and when it was to happen.

The four were in an ideal position. Both clubs wanted them. There was nothing to bind them to Ottawa. They were free agents. The "reserve clause" or "option clause" was not part of any agreements signed. In reality, nothing had been signed with Ottawa anyway. All operated as gentlemen. A handshake was sufficient.

Renfrew withdrew, confident that the players would see their way to continue the negotiations with them. Ottawa presented their case. For the better part of the day, the players went back and forth between the two clubs, looking for the best deal. In the end, "after a fierce lot of bidding,"[4] the gang of four decided to remain with Ottawa. No terms were announced but contracts of two thousand dollars were rumoured to be the Ottawa settlement. More importantly, the civil service was a factor. All were to have good positions in the Ottawa bureaucracy.

Among the Renfrew owners, there was a curious sense of enthusiasm. They had come close. They had not signed the four but they had rattled Ottawa; they had caused their salaries to escalate, putting pressure on the whole of the Canadian League. Other players would want to be paid similarly; gate receipts would have to be high indeed. It might have been a Pyrrhic victory:

*Ottawa has won out in the greatest battle for players Canada has ever witnessed but the victory has been a costly one. How much will it cost the Ottawas to hold the team together for one season is a matter of conjecture. The figures will not be greatly less than the sum would have cost Renfrew had every offer been accepted. All Canada is flushed with amazement at the fight for Ottawa players that the Renfrew aggregation backed by a few millionaires has been waging.* [5]

It was obvious that Renfrew was not counting on its population or arena capacity to generate the money needed. Fifteen thousand dollars was set aside for hockey with little hope of getting it back through gate receipts. With some awe, it was reported that the money offered to Kerr, Walsh, Lake and Taylor was "larger in proportion to the work and time required than those required by the National and American baseball league stars."[6]

From the players, however, aware of the possibility that their careers could be ended at any time, or, their earning power suddenly disappear, there was certainly no apology tendered. Marty Walsh seemed to be speaking for all of them when he defended his attempt to get the best deal for himself:

*Two hundred dollars a week for hockey seems easy money, but, I can tell you when a man draws that amount, he pretty nearly earns every cent of it. Take myself for instance. I have only played pro hockey for a comparatively short time. Yet, I have taken some lumps and it takes a lot of money to equalize. My first year, I was handed a broken ankle at the Soo which laid me on my back for about six weeks. That was worth something. Then in New York, last year, I came out of the game with a face that looked like the results of an encounter with wild cats. I had all my front teeth knocked out and it cost money to get new ones. . . .* [7]

Typical of the situation was the case of Edgar Dey, another member of the Ottawa 1909 Stanley Cup champions. Travelling to Montreal, at the request of the Montreal Wanderers' Dickie Boon, the announcement was made that he had agreed to terms with the Montreal team and would sign with them. The NHA seemed determined to disrupt the Canadian League and Ottawa was its prime target. One week later, however, Dey surfaced in Renfrew. Obviously attracted by the contracts offered to his team-mates, he indicated that he was ready to sign with the Creamery Kings. The next day, after some contact with Cobalt, he was reported to have agreed to one thousand dollars to play there. That evening, he bettered himself, once again, by accepting an offer from Haileybury, his pay calling for twelve hundred dollars for the season. He was given an additional bonus of one hundred dollars "to bind the agreement."[8] All the NHA clubs were upset. After all, they were driving their own costs up; the idea was to drive up the costs of the other league and make it difficult for them to operate! Renfrew was particularly incensed, "threatening to bar Dey altogether."[9] "He must be something of a lady to coquette with all those clubs,"[10] tut-tutted *The Renfrew Journal.*

To insinuations that it served them right for trying to steal Ottawa's players, Renfrew's George Martel responded:

*We are not stealing the Ottawa players. All the dickering has been above-board and open. Before we talked business with them, we first asked each player to go to the Ottawa Club and tell their officers that they had been approached by us and not until the Ottawa Club had made their terms to any of the players did we make our offers. We want the very best team money can buy, the best team in the world, in fact. And we don't care where it comes from. We are after the Ottawa men because we think that they are the best in the country.* [11]

Perhaps fearful of what was going to happen next, the Ottawa *Citizen*, aware of all the turmoil that had erupted and wary of the outcome, concluded thoughtfully: "Renfrew should have been admitted."[12]

Rumours continued to swirl about. A breathless newspaper story reported that Ottawa, and the Montreal Shamrocks, were contemplating moving from the Canadian to the National. The story went on to furnish "proof": Renfrew had given up too easily in trying to sign the Ottawa four; if they were really serious in rendering Ottawa ineffective, that was their chance. "Renfrew gave up on the fight for the Ottawa stars in a very tame sort of manner, indicating again that there has to be a shuffle somewhere."[13] The story was potentially disruptive enough that Vice-President Sparks personally went to the *Journal* offices to deny the story on Ottawa's behalf.

Meanwhile, Renfrew continued to work on its "fifteen thousand dollar team."[14] Out of the blue, it announced that it had signed "two of the finest players in the game,"[15] Lester and Frank Patrick. Their signing was a cause for celebration in Renfrew and awe throughout the rest of the hockey world - yet another indication of the length to which the Renfrew millionaires were set to go to in order to gain the Stanley Cup.

The Patricks had been a fixture around Montreal and Ottawa circles, Frank with the amateur Victorias and McGill, while Lester had been a member of the successful Stanley Cup Wanderer teams of 1906 and 1907, as well as the unsuccessful representatives from Brandon in 1904 and Edmonton in 1909. The two had moved to Nelson, B.C. , where the father of the hockey-playing family, Joe, owned a profitable lumber business. A combination of depressed conditions on the Canadian prairies and the search for hockey talent in central Canada caused the Patricks to be inundated with offers. It seemed as if every team in the country was after them. They would be the difference between an also-ran and a Stanley Cup champion.

Perhaps the toughest person to sell on the boys' return to hockey, and professional hockey at that, was Joe, a staunch Irish protestant lumberman who was always aware of the temptations that might corrupt the members of his family. Both Ottawa and the Montreal Wanderers were after Lester, as was Edmonton. News reports of the day kept track of the two celebrities as they made their way from Nelson, British Columbia, eastward. Lester was in Calgary; Frank was on his way to Montreal, preferring to play as an amateur with the Victorias; Lester was in Edmonton as manager of the team going east to challenge for the Stanley Cup, one of his first duties, to sign brother Frank. . . [16]

Therefore, it was an unexpected shock to almost all, and especially the Ottawa followers, when the news was released that Renfrew had signed the Patricks. *The Gazette* carried the story with a banner proclaiming: "highest price yet."[17] The Patricks were to receive three thousand dollars each! According to the Edmonton *Bulletin*, Ottawa was to blame for Edmonton's loss of the Patricks. They had signed with the western team on the understanding that Edmonton's Stanley Cup challenge with Ottawa would be prior to December 11. If not, the two were free to negotiate with whomever they wished.

Replying to a wire from M.J. O'Brien, Lester had matter-of-factly replied that he would be willing to come to Renfrew for three thousand dollars plus expenses for a twelve-game season. It was a gamble on Patrick's part; he had not asked for more than eighteen hundred dollars from any other team that had contacted him. To his astonishment, O'Brien agreed. . . and when inquiries were made as to the availability of Frank, Lester matter-of-factly mentioned that, yes, he was - at a cost of two thousand dollars! Again, O'Brien assented, obviously enthralled at the prospect of having the two superstars join his team. Renfrew continued to be the talk of the country.

*How pursued had the Patrick brothers been? Over a two-week period, twenty-six wires were received from six different teams. "One wire was delivered to the house on Sunday", recalled Frank, "and my father refused to accept it. But after church, Lester sneaked over to the telegraph office and obtained it. It was the original wire from the Renfrew people."[18]*

To Montreal Shamrocks president Lunny, the money spent by Renfrew was "lunacy. . . profligate spending and if continued, will ruin hockey."[19] Of course, the Shamrocks were in the rival league; they could see their gates being torn away and rushing to the Wanderers, and their players were going to be demanding higher salaries once they saw how much the Patricks were being paid.

While western papers mourned the loss of the Patricks, those in the east were joyous, almost in awe of this hockey team that was being put together in the backwoods farming town of Renfrew. There was recognition that the town was "in a fever of excitement. . . people here talk of little else."[20] The bidding, the salaries, the personalities notwithstanding, the *Journal* mused, the fact remained that when Renfrew's arena capacity was taken into account with the price of tickets and the number of games, it was impossible that the club would make money. The Patricks alone would account for half the gate receipts!

Ottawa papers, particularly, seemed almost paranoid whenever a member of the Renfrew delegation appeared in the Stanley Cup city. At the very moment when the Patricks' signing was being announced, George Martel was reported in Ottawa. The focus turned to the Ottawa players again, particularly Taylor, and the notion of benign millionaire owners supplying an endless amount of cash and putting Renfrew on the map:

*Mr. M.J. O'Brien and his partner, Mr. J. George Barnet, are said to know little of the team's make-up. They have furnished the "wherewithal" and furnished it without stint but they are generally credited with knowing little of the doings of their agent, or for that matter, of hockey, as the town's humblest shoe-shine boy. It would take something of a strange crystal-gazer to see a man like O'Brien, who has built his fortune by his own power of mind and limitless energy, sinking many thousands into a wild goldbrick scheme, or Mr. Barnet, either. It is therefore safe to assume that they know a lot more about the team than what they read in the papers and that the team is one that is really going to put Renfrew on the map.* [21]

Indeed, it was obvious that O'Brien was more aware of the hockey goings-on than was generally believed. True, he had given out the order to sign the best players that could be found but he also wanted to be fully apprised of developments. When the club announced the signing of Herb Jordan, a speedy centre from Quebec, it was also stated that he preferred to play as an amateur. It wasn't that Renfrew was trying to save money, many players of the day preferred to retain their amateur status. And Jordan was an established star in his own right, too. He had been the second leading scorer in the ECHA the past season, scoring thirty goals in the twelve-game season - and all the while playing with a last-place team.

O'Brien showed his flexibility. Not wanting to leave any stone unturned in his attempt to assemble the best players he could, and his money not being directly of use in this situation, the mining magnate used his business interests to lure Jordan. He needed a private secretary. Jordan had some expertise in this area. O'Brien, in effect, offered Jordan a personal-services contract. Jordan accepted and for many years he was to act on O'Brien's behalf in various interests. Among other initiatives, Jordan was involved in operating a theatre in 1912, showing two-reel films for an admission of ten cents, was on the Board of Directors of Renfrew Machinery, and helped found the Renfrew Golf Club in 1929.

Certainly, Jordan did not have the high profile of the Patricks or of Fred Taylor, but that soon became immaterial. Once he was announced as a member of the Renfrew aggregation, fast becoming *the* topic of conversation, importance was ascribed to him.

There was an amusing anecdote concerning Jordan, his new team and the amateur Rivers, Renfrew's other less-publicized, but still well-known hockey team that was in danger of being somewhat lost in the enthusiasm for O'Brien's Valley boys. Indeed the Rivers were unwilling or unable to schedule their games until the NHA did so with its dates. As a result, they were unable to generate as much publicity as they would have liked.

Regardless, keen followers, especially young impressionable boys, seemed to be aware of every detail that was transpiring:

*At a local Sunday School class last Sunday, the teacher in the class was giving a splendid description of the river Jordan. Noticing that one young man was inattentive, the teacher sought to catch him napping by suddenly turning to him and asking: "and now, what is Jordan?" "A hockey player", was the prompt but unaccepted reply. "Oh no", said the teacher, "will; someone who has been paying attention give us the correct answer?"*

*"Jordan is one of the rivers", began another scholar in response but he was quickly interrupted by the first boy. "He isn't one of the Rivers at all. He plays centre for the Seniors."*[22]

Ever aware that Renfrew agents were lurking in their city ready to abscond with their prized players, the *Citizen* reported, somewhat ominously, that Taylor was still not out with the Stanley Cup champions; a cold was labelled as the culprit. When, at the next practice, Taylor still had not appeared, the cause was pin-pointed as a misunderstanding. Taylor had requested a favour; the club had agreed. Taylor declared that to be fine; he would attend practice when the favour was carried out. "The Ottawas thought that they had granted his request but through a mistake, Taylor was left under the wrong impression,"[23] and the club directors met; the misunderstanding was resolved. Taylor was to make his first appearance at an Ottawa practice for the upcoming season. It appeared that he was becoming somewhat peeved by the hearsay which continued to circulate about him: "Please don't couple my name with Renfrew again. I have not seen any of them for over a week. They won't want me now anyways."[24]

All of this was under the heading "Will Renfrew Never Let Up?" If Ottawa supporters had the feeling that there was a concerted effort under way to sabotage their team, they could have been excused. "Renfrew Sports Have The Nerve,"[25] headed yet another account of a frontal assault described in detail. Renfrew was proposing to operate excursions from Ottawa to Renfrew for its games. Ottawa saw it as yet another incursion on their territory. First they were after every member of the Ottawa team; now they were trying to coax fans from the capital.

It wasn't sabotage, retorted George Barnet, just good practice. The Renfrew partner was at the Russell House in Ottawa, telling all who would listen, especially the inquiring media, with a straight face: "We have almost as many supporters in Ottawa as we have in our own town. We have been requested by scores of people in the Capital to reserve some seats, to arrange some excursions. Our season-tickets will be gobbled up in no time but we will not forget our Ottawa friends for whom we'll lay a full section aside."[26]

Reports were continuing to circulate that Ottawa money was now finding its way to Renfrew to back that team in its search for players, that special excursions from Ottawa would be arranged for games with the Wanderers and the Canadiens, and that exhibition games would take place in Dusquesne Gardens in Pittsburgh as well as in New York, to show people there how hockey should be played on their fancy artificial rinks.

And more rumours about Taylor, always Taylor.

When an Ottawa follower informed the hockey club that he had seen Taylor at the station shortly after the Renfrew train had pulled out, another was positive that Taylor had been on it. And by coincidence certainly,the club was assured, George Martel was in town. As reporters rushed to Martel to inquire about the Cyclone, the Renfrew man simply stated that Taylor had been left alone since he informed them that he would rather stay in Ottawa. As always, though, Martel and Renfrew left the door open saying they would be willing to "give him any amount to get him there."[27]

The salaries offered were still the number-one topic in hockey circles. The Montreal *Gazette*, as incredulous as many other followers of the national pastime, wondered, much in the same fashion that future followers of the game would when discussing the escalating salaries of the current players: "What would Russell Bowie be worth to Renfrew?"[28] It was a reference to the recently retired scoring ace of the Montreal Victorias who was ranked by many as the greatest centre in the game, perhaps for all time but certainly that the game had known so far. During the eighty scheduled games he had played, he had scored the unheard-of total of two hundred and thirty-four goals or an average of almost three goals for every match played. [29]

And in Ottawa, even though their players had rejected Renfrew's offers, it was still the main dressing-room topic. Marty Walsh lamented that he didn't " want to see those Renfrew magnates anymore". . . they kept him awake at night "thinking of all the coin (he had) turned down."[30] Whenever the Ottawa players wanted a good laugh, one would wonder aloud why Renfrew hadn't offered Bad Joe Hall a contract. Hall was the acknowledged enforcer of hockey; his name always accompanied by the epithet Bad or Mean, seldom simply Joe Hall. There was a spate of stories circulating about him. He was said to have been a bit of a hooligan as a youngster. When one of his "friends," Bill Miner, "broke into the safe-cracking business, Joe took up hockey as a profession."[31] Born in England, he played with teams in Winnipeg, Brandon, Kenora, Quebec and Montreal gaining a reputation as "the bad man of the game for the reason that he had a long list of knock-outs to his record in the hockey pastime."[32] Somewhat of a legend in his own time, Hall was liable to show up at half-time of a match sporting his oiled black hair and shiny black boots. Players would laugh uproariously at stories told at his expense; in one, he was said to have told his new team-mates that he was the most popular player ever to have played in Brandon and when the train pulled into the station, he was sure that the depot would be jammed with his followers. On arrival, however, the station was deserted; Hall was never allowed to forget it and the story became one of the most told and retold wherever players gathered. Only a shout of "Where's Joe Hall?" was needed to trigger it once again. [33]

Perhaps the Ottawa *Citizen* was right when it wrote that the "cry of 'Renfrew' is becoming worse than 'wolf' to the Ottawa Hockey Club."[34] Once again headlines erupted from the newspaper: "Renfrew Officers Claim Taylor." The story went on to state that the Cyclone had signed the previous evening, Friday, with the creamery town for three thousand dollars and a position for the season. Renfrew officers confirmed it. The Listowel Phenom declined to make a definite statement, but, as far as the newspaper was concerned, he "practically admitted that he had changed his allegiance from Ottawa to Renfrew."[35]

As if to uncover some reason as to why it might not be so, the newspaper retraced the events. There was the familiar conjecture that it was or was not a question of finances; that it was or was not a matter of a position outside hockey; that it was or was not a promise that the club had made. Taylor had gone to Renfrew Thursday night, and returned Friday, to meet at the Windsor Hotel for three hours with M.J. , George Martel, Larry Gilmour and Thomas Low, MP, all members of the Renfrew executive. Shortly after eleven, the paper reported, all details had been worked out; Taylor signed. Only one detail was left to be cleared up: "a provision attached to his contract and it is up to Renfrew to make good a promise before Taylor will budge from Ottawa."[36]

The staggering sum of three thousand dollars was mentioned, in addition to a position which would allow Taylor to continue living in Ottawa.

It seemed as if all hell had broken loose. Marty Walsh and Albert Kerr were approached once more. Taylor met with his Ottawa mates and was reported to have told them that "there is more glory and money to be paid in the National League."[37] The evening edition of the *Citizen* seemed to be losing its patience. It decried the developing "hockey farce comedy with Renfrew saying that they have Taylor, Ottawa saying that he's going to stay there and Taylor doesn't know."[38] Meanwhile, Taylor was to practise with the Ottawa team on Saturday night, a move which caused Renfrew officials to wonder whether they had been used once again. Taylor, an employee of the Interior Department, had been promised by the Ottawa club that they would do all that they could do to guarantee a promotion. "A special examination was said to have been arranged for him through the intercessions of some very influential members of Parliament." To counter this, O'Brien, with the assistance of Thomas Low, MP, came up with another government position, "in the outside service, which had been held open for a Renfrew man. It was waiting for Taylor to step into."[39]

As if to underscore the treasure that was Taylor, the *Citizen* mused:

*There are many hockey players but there is only one Taylor. No one but he can stride along in such a manner that the opposing defencemen are unable to get close enough to block him. Taylor's big asset is his peculiar style of skating and his great speed. Before starting, he curves across the ice and gets an impetus and by that time, he has reached the waiting defence. He is going at such a rate that he can step out of the way and pass them without giving them a chance. His pace is such that he is able to carry the puck for a long time, holding his stick in one hand, a stunt which is out of the question for the average players who must withstand the check with the stick held in two hands.*[40]

As before, the sentimental goodbyes were premature. That same evening, Saturday, December 18, the man in question was at the Ottawa practice, much to the delight of the throng who had come out to see for themselves. It was a vintage Taylor who, the *Journal* opined, "would add much to his reputation as a hockey whirlwind, playing as he did in practice Saturday night."[41] Monday's *Citizen* breathlessly informed its readers of the latest in the continuing saga: the agreement which Taylor had signed contained a proviso. If Ottawa was able to satisfy his demands, he was free to ignore the contract and stay with them. It was a calculated gamble which Renfrew had taken but one which players loved since they had leverage which would allow them to obtain the best terms possible. There were reports that Renfrew would take legal action. Not at all, stated one official, taking the high road, "Taylor's contract was to be destroyed, nothing further done. We did our best to get Taylor but his love for Ottawa is apparently too strong. We will not make a further offer to get him."[42]

Collectively, the Ottawa team and its supporters could almost be heard to breathe a sigh of relief. Indeed, they began to breathe more easily when the revered cover-point himself said: "Yes, I did sign a Renfrew contract but later developments convinced me that it would be in my best interests to stay with the local club and that is what I intend to do."[43]

On the surface, a calm seemed to descend upon the hockey goings-on. Fans in Ottawa and Renfrew began to busy themselves with thoughts of other things. The hockey situation seemed to be sorting itself out as it should be, and Christmas was coming very quickly. Yet there was still a nagging doubt in Ottawa. After all, they had gone through all of this many times before since Renfrew burst on to the scene with its disruptive tactics. The Ottawa club had heard it all before too and when Lester Patrick was seen at the train station in Ottawa, the feeling of panic returned. The *Citizen*, alerted by a concerned club supporter, interviewed the newly arrived Renfrew star, asking the reason for his surprise visit to Ottawa. The nonchalant visitor remarked that it was December 21, four days before Christmas; he had some last minute shopping to do. "Fred Taylor, Albert Kerr and Marty Walsh might prove pretty expensive gifts from Santa Claus to the Renfrew Club," one wag suggested. "Patrick wouldn't admit that he had any such intentions."[44]

The Patricks were the darlings of the hockey public everywhere, their reputation preceding them wherever they went. Stories about Lester's good nature and ability to entertain made the rounds. People from Montreal to Nelson were familiar with the talent the superstar had in singing and his recital of "Little Bateese" with his lumberjack French. He was the quintessential modest, unassuming star, just beginning to appreciate his value as a player in the early days of the professional game of hockey. When he first moved to Nelson, he was asked to play for the Victorias as a rover; he scored all five goals in the team's victory. The former Montreal Wanderer was asked to join Edmonton. It was 1907 and the western city was challenging the Montreal Wanderers for the Cup. After first receiving permission from his father, he accepted and made his way to Montreal to play with his new team-mates, including Bert Lindsay, Didier Pitre, Tom Phillips and Fred Whitcroft, a veritable who's who of current players. The Wanderers were intact from the year before with the addition of Art Ross to replace Patrick.  After the series, won by the Wanderers, Ross and Patrick dined together.

*"Lester", said Ross, "how much did they pay you for the series?"*

*"Just expenses," said Lester, "Why?"*

*"Why?", snorted Ross. "Do you know what kind of money we're getting now in the east to play hockey?" . . . Ross had held out for the outlandish sum of $1600. but settled for $1200. "I got four hundred dollars for this series", said Ross. "In advance!"*

*He reached into his pocket, pulled out a wad of bills and counted them out on the table.*

*"And I was cheated too!" he continued, "Phillips got six hundred from Edmonton and played less than half a game. Lester, you are a dumkopf."*

*Ross allowed the dumkopf to pick up the dinner check. After all, Lester was getting expenses.*

*When Lester got back to Nelson, his father asked him how much the trip had cost, rail fare, meals, hotel and all.*

*"Sixty-two dollars", said Lester.*

*"How much expense money did you get?"*

*"One hundred dollars."*

*"Then, you owe Edmonton thirty-eight dollars."*

*Lester sent a check for that amount."*[45]

Now, in the closing weeks of 1909, when Renfrew was holding its opening practice for the 1910 season at the Argyle Street rink, fully five hundred townspeople, more than fifteen per cent of the population, came to watch the team whose name was on everybody's lips. While they mourned the loss of one they thought they had, Fred Taylor, nonetheless, "Lester and Frank Patrick delighted the railbirds with their beautiful stick handling and skating."[46]

The "one hundred thousand dollars worth of advertising Renfrew has received through an effort to gather a championship hockey team,"[47]continued. *The Globe* featured the Patricks in a lengthy article, complete with pictures, and a headline: "Renfrew's Five Thousand Dollar Beauties." A full description in glowing terms featured the more-than-six-foot-tall Lester and the twenty-five-year-old, one-hundred-eighty-pound Frank, the latter being named the best defenceman in hockey "excepting, perhaps, Taylor of Ottawa."[48]

In keeping with the season, Ottawa supporters might have expected that they would have been spared further Renfrew sorties into their territory. It was not to be. On Christmas Day itself, Renfrew officials were reported to have been in the city to help plan and organize a new club, the All Ottawas, "to be operated in direct opposition to the Ottawa Club."[49] It was to be composed of all home-town players. More importantly, however, the new volley of speculation signalled a new escalation in the continuing battle between the NHA and the CHL and particularly, between Renfrew and Ottawa. Moreover, it was leaked that the Stanley Cup-champion Ottawa club was still attempting to gain admittance to the upstart new league, if not for the present season, then definitely for 1910/11. Ottawa hockey fans simply did not know what to make of all this. They only knew that there would be good hockey this season, and lots of it. When the Renfrew team further announced that they, and the Wanderers, were endeavouring to play an exhibition game in Ottawa on New Year's Day, 1910, reports read,"the people here (Ottawa) are crazy with excitement. . . the match would pack the arena. . . popularize the National Hockey League."[50]

The Ottawa club understood that it was all a ploy to undercut them; they controlled the arena. They made a counter-offer: Renfrew versus Ottawa, a prize trophy worth two hundred dollars and bragging rights to the winner. Indeed, seeking the initiative, Ottawa suggested that the winner take all the gate receipts! Renfrew wasn't biting. They replied that when they played Ottawa, there would be more than a two-hundred-dollar trophy at stake! There would be no exhibition game under any circumstances "because of the way they were treated in connection with their Stanley Cup challenge."[51]

Ottawa continued the war of words, mounting a concerted counter-attack. They hinted, "Sunday games would be played by the National League teams."[52] Predictably, Renfrew lost no time in denying the charge and hitting back at the source: "the rumours about Sunday games have been started by people with the intention of hurting the National League. . . not for a minute would we tolerate. . . to desecrate the Sabbath."[53] It was much like a table-tennis match with the charges and counter-charges rebounding back and forth. Battle lines were drawn and redrawn. When the *Citizen* printed a story about former Brandon player, Jack Fraser, who arrived in the East looking for a team to play with, the headline caption was: "Watch Them Grab Him."[54] No explanation of *them* was necessary. Indeed the *them* was on everybody's mind - and would be even more so in the days to come!

As the year came to a close, the Ottawa papers, once again, wailed: "Taylor's in Renfrew - Jumped Ottawa Yesterday."[55] It was true. The man they called the Tornado in Portage, Whirlwind in Houghton and Cyclone in Ottawa had made the move to Renfrew, once again, some cynics were to say.

But this time,it was for keeps. M.J. O'Brien, who had always spoken of Taylor as his first priority, had won!

*The Renfrew Journal* continued the war, not so gently teasing the Ottawa citizens for their figurative "robes of black."[56] Renfrew citizens were wearing anything but black as they celebrated the belated Christmas present heralding the new year. Fully one thousand came out to the rink to watch the Renfrew practice and "the Listowel boy proceeded to give an exhibition of stunts which had made him the idol of Ottawa."[57] Taylor had arrived from Ottawa on the five-o'clock train with George Martel, and was escorted to the rink in time for the seven-o'clock practice. "The one thousand railbirds thronged the rink and Taylor was given a great reception when he skated out, garbed for the first time in a Renfrew sweater."[58]

If Taylor were playing today, he would be classed as a franchise player, an Orr, Esposito, Gretzky or Lemieux in another era. Already in 1909, he was a legend in the making, a consummate artist on skates amidst the violence and mayhem that could be hockey. Followers of the game were familiar with the young, prematurely balding man; newcomers to the game were attracted by the huge amounts of publicity which he generated. His story[59] was becoming a well-known one. He was born in Tara, Ontario, and christened Frederick Wellington. By age seventeen he had led his Listowel Minto team to a second league championship, quit school and worked in a piano factory for five dollars a week. As an eighteen-year-old, in 1902, he was asked to play in an exhibition series in Houghton, Michigan, then a burgeoning venue for the game. His play attracted much attention among hockey people in Ontario and in the autumn of 1903 he received a phone call from W.A. Hewitt, inviting him to play for the Toronto Marlboros. Such a big city frightened him. He preferred the smaller, more rural communities and so, he declined. Hewitt was persistent, Taylor as much so. Hewitt, in keeping with the amateur-control reality of the times, informed Taylor that if he refused to play for Toronto, he wouldn't play anywhere! The Ontario Hockey Association, claiming that Taylor had violated his amateur status by playing in Houghton, carried out Hewitt's threat. Taylor was barred from playing with Listowel and with a team in far-away Thessalon, which, unaware of the situation, had invited him to be part of their club. They were forced to either drop the youngster or be banned themselves.

In 1905, Taylor moved west from Ontario to Portage la Prairie, Manitoba. He was twenty years old, had been forced to sit out of hockey the previous year, and was moving into senior hockey, somewhat nervously, for the first time. His contract was modest, but in keeping with the time: room and board, a train ticket and twenty-five dollars a month pocket-money. He was an immediate hit, the Portage la Prairie people dubbing him a tornado. His impressive play caused the Kenora (previously known as Rat Portage) Thistles to ask him to join them in their quest to gain the Stanley Cup from the Wanderers. Taylor declined. Instead, he joined the Portage Lake team of Houghton in the International Professional League, the first league to openly declare itself so. Taylor was able to arrange to drop his commitments to the Manitoba and

Kenora teams and accept the Houghton offer of four hundred dollars plus expenses for the remainder of the season.

It was a bitterly cold Manitoba morning when the youngster left, travelling south to change trains at the American border. Taylor had a telegram confirming that he had a job in Houghton but it was no guarantee that he would be allowed into the United States. However, that and his reputation as a hockey player, and the good fortune that one of the U.S. immigration inspectors had seen Taylor play in Winnipeg, assured him of no problems. The inspector even bought him a cup of coffee and engaged him in a spirited conversation about hockey, obviously enjoying the impressive Canadian export.

His two years at Houghton were rewarded with his selection to the all-star team for his whirlwind performances, two championships, the scoring leadership and so much publicity that he was as well-known in the northern United States as he was in Manitoba and Ontario.

Taylor would have been content to stay in Houghton, but a recession and declining copper prices hit the mining community. As the winter of 1907 approached, Houghton decided to disband its championship team. Players such as Taylor, Newsy Lalonde, Hod Stuart, Riley Hern and Marty Walsh were eagerly sought-after. Taylor said he felt "like a bride with two handsome suitors."[60]

Indeed, there were letters and visitors arriving by train regularly during the summer of 1907 at the small community of Listowel; all sought to sign the rising young superstar. Riley Hern appeared from Montreal. Malcolm Brice, the well-known sports editor of *The Ottawa Free Press*, also came, offering Taylor five hundred dollars for the ten-game season plus a job with the civil service's immigration department. It was also the first time that Taylor had come across the name of M.J. O'Brien. A bid came from Cobalt, a town of three thousand, which appealed to Taylor. Much like Houghton, it was a mining community, its reputation and future resting on the huge silver deposits owned, in part, by M.J. O'Brien. The big, bearded Irishman had one ambition in hockey - to win the Stanley Cup - and he intended to use the property at Cobalt as the magnet to attract top hockey players.

But Taylor wasn't ready, yet, to join the O'Briens in their quest. He accepted the Ottawa offer, as much for the steady job as anything. Yet the story circulated as to how the brash, raw youngster almost never got the civil-service position. When Taylor arrived at the offices of the Hon. Frank Oliver, the Minister of the Interior in the Liberal government, he was accompanied by the Ottawa Club directors. Oliver had a reputation as a tough, no-nonsense, very blunt westerner. He asked Taylor if he had a letter of recommendation from his Member of Parliament. The response left the minister blustering: "Mr. Minister, I didn't know anything about such a letter, but I couldn't have gotten one anyway. Our MP is Mr. Rankin. Now, he's probably a nice enough fellow, but unfortunately, he's a Liberal. Our family wouldn't go anywhere near him."[61]

Such was the power of hockey in Ottawa that Taylor was awarded the thirty-five-dollar-a-week position and a spot with the famed Ottawa Senators Hockey Club. His play quickly received rave notices. . . and repeated overtures from the O'Brien interests. The more that they saw of him, the more they were convinced that they had to have him on any Stanley Cup challenge they could put together. Taylor's dashing style even attracted the notice of the Governor General, Earl Grey, who was responsible for yet another Taylor sobriquet: "that new number 4, Taylor, he's a cyclone if I ever saw one."[62] Grey's daughter was similarly in awe. She requested one of the Cyclone's sticks. "It cost him $1. 50 for another one but he figured it was worth it."[63] Years later, Taylor met the daughter in London; she still had the stick.

It was at the immigration offices that Taylor met a young lady, Thirza Cook. She was from a wealthy family that didn't take kindly to the young hockey player. Sensing the discouragement from her mother, Taylor privately vowed that he would have a bank account of ten thousand dollars before he asked for Thirza's hand in marriage. At a time when a good suit cost fifteen dollars, a meal twenty-five cents, a good pair of shoes, three dollars, ten thousand dollars was a small fortune; but the love-struck hockey player was bound to get it. . . and hockey was his only vehicle. . . .

And so, when the ever-pursuing Renfrew executive, once again, had their quarry, they were bound and determined that the third time would be lucky. George Martel booked himself into Ottawa's Windsor Hotel, O'Brien's headquarters in that city, on December 28. Immediately, he contacted Taylor and requested a meeting. Taylor agreed. He sensed that it would be his last chance to do better for himself. He asked for and received permission to be accompanied by a good friend, Jack McGinnis, a teacher who lived in Taylor's boarding-house. McGinnis was a prototype agent; he was to do all the talking and get the best deal that he could. For his part, Martel also knew that this was his last chance. He didn't want it to slip by or to have any agreement he might make upstaged by Ottawa.

When the three met, there were some rather open statements being made. Taylor simply sat back and listened to the two gentlemen discussing his future. McGinnis opened by suggesting that any contract should immediately recognize that Taylor should be the highest-paid player in the league, that he should also have a position outside hockey at least equal to the one he had in Ottawa. Martel nodded thoughtfully. He was quite willing to spend the money but, twice previously, Taylor had simply used the negotiations with Renfrew to better himself financially with Ottawa. A guarantee was needed to ensure that this would not happen again. Who proposed it is not known, but the idea of a one-thousand-dollar performance bond was raised. If Taylor would sign a contract and post a bond for one thousand dollars, to be forfeited if he backtracked, the talks could continue. McGinnis had a further twist: Taylor would post the bond but, if he kept his contract, the Renfrew team would match the one thousand dollars!

Taylor followed the conversation of the two men who sat opposite each other, leaning intently. Martel nodded, not wanting to agree until the contract itself had been discussed. Sensing this, McGinnis moved to the contract. Firstly, he said, Taylor should be the highest-paid player on the team. Martel said that would be no problem. Lester Patrick was earning three thousand dollars; if Taylor satisfied the contractual discussion, he would earn more than that. Again McGinnis, wanting no loose ends, spoke. According to his calculations the total contract, bond and position, totalled five thousand, two hundred and fifty dollars. Taylor's eyes widened; Martel nodded slowly, wanting to make sure that there were to be no further demands before he agreed. McGinnis continued: the entire amount should be held in trust in Taylor's name in Taylor's Ottawa bank before the beginning of the season, but not to be drawn on until the end of it.

When Martel agreed and the contract was signed, Fred "Cyclone" Taylor became the highest-paid athlete in Canada and, on a per-game basis, in the world. He was being paid five thousand, two hundred and fifty dollars for a twelve-game season over two months. Ty Cobb, the great American baseball player, had recently signed for six thousand, five hundred dollars. That was over seven months and one hundred and fifty-four games!

The signing completed, Taylor and Martel made arrangements to meet and return to Renfrew where a jubilant executive and town awaited its newest conquering hero. As for the immediate present, however, Taylor and McGinnis, both teetotallers, celebrated "with a couple of very nice ice-cream sodas."[64] To all concerned, except the Ottawas of course, it was a glorious way to end 1909 and a grand beginning to 1910.

# *Chapter Four*

## *. . . Join Them!*

There were the usual number of parties in both Ottawa and Renfrew as the new year of 1910 made its appearance. It was also cold: 5°F in Ottawa, -4°F in Renfrew. The Ottawa citizenry seemed to be more aware of the weather, the Renfrewites, oblivious. The revellers in Ottawa seemed almost subdued, listless, spiritless; the wind had been taken out of their sails. In Renfrew, a fresh breeze of promise seemed everywhere. The Cyclone was spoken of everywhere. In Ottawa, it was a mournful reminiscence, a sense of loss, not only for Taylor but also for the Stanley Cup. In Renfrew, the love affair with O'Brien and his hockey team had become even more enhanced. The small community saw the cold weather as a guarantee of the keen ice necessary to allow the town's hockey team to display its abundant skills to the fullest.

It was a love affair, and togetherness was the watchword. Togetherness for O'Brien and his team, the town and the team, and the team members among themselves. The O'Briens hosted a combination Christmas/New Year's dinner for the team: Lester and Frank Patrick, Cyclone Taylor, Bert Lindsay, Herb Jordan, Larry Gilmour and Bobby Rowe. Later, there would be more block-buster signings but it was this group of seven who were now brought together in an attempt to promote team unity, friendship, knowledge of each other as individuals, and to allow M.J. and his family to be gracious patrons. O'Brien lived in a huge mansion on Barr Street. In the grand way that was M.J.'s, he had taken a one-floor house, raised the roof and added a gallery with bedrooms running off it on the second floor, and three more rooms on the third. Downstairs were the kitchen, dining-room, drawing-room, and den. The players were in awe of the surroundings, but not as much as O'Brien's children were of them. Ambrose, Mary Stella, Mary Jamesina, Mary Grace, Jack, Patrick and Mary Gertrude - the youngest, five, the eldest, twenty-five - hung on every word spoken by the dashing young crusaders in search of the Holy Grail that was the Stanley Cup. Champagne flowed, literally and in spirit, since the Patricks and Taylor were non-drinkers. Conversation was loud, spontaneous and joyous. Everyone was pleased that the others were part of the scene. And just to ensure that some hockey news was available for the town's consumption, Ambrose O'Brien announced to all that the captain of the Renfrew team would be Lester Patrick. It wasn't his first such honour. He had previously held the same position with the Montreal Wanderers when they had won the Stanley Cup; hopefully, history would repeat itself.

The social flurry of activity continued for the magnificent seven. Winter was a time to get out and challenge the elements. Practices were interspersed with "sleighing parties, snowshoe parties, skating parties and just plain parties."[1]

The players seemed to be everywhere together. The Patricks, Taylor, Lindsay and Rowe all stayed at the same Renfrew boarding-house. Each dinner meal was an opportunity to have an informal team meeting. Occasionally, there was some light banter with Lester, the life of the party, telling stories or reciting poetry in French. Frank was somewhat quieter, withdrawn in comparison with his more outgoing and gregarious brother, but when the conversation turned to hockey, he was suddenly animated, ready to advance his ideas on how the game could be improved or how tactics could be developed to take full advantage of the game as it was.

It also gave the players a chance to become familiar with each other. Taylor and the Patricks were well-known through all the publicity they had always received. Lindsay, Rowe, Jordan and Gilmour were becoming accustomed to the increased glare of the spotlight.

Lindsay, who first played in Guelph as an amateur, joined the professional ranks with the Guelph Nationals in the Ontario Professional League, moving later to the Toronto Argonauts and Edmonton, when they challenged for the Stanley Cup. He had spent eleven years on a cattle ranch in Montana, which "doubtless gave him that cool daring and quick eye. . . and his cool indifference to the wicked onslaught of opponents' forwards."[2]

Bobby Rowe was born in Heathcote, Ontario, playing senior hockey in the OHA at Barrie, Ontario, before leaving to join Houghton of the International Professional League. He was a favourite with the Renfrew fans because of his persistence and his ability to "play his check to the finish every time."[3]

Larry Gilmour was considered a homebrew even though he was born in nearby Almonte. He had lived in Renfrew for years and seemed to have played every position with the team. He was valuable: strong defensively but "with no peers at forward."[4] He had played with the Soo in the International League and later with the Wanderers when they needed a cover-point. Gilmour, however, a husky young man known for his "hurdling dashes down the ice,"[5] spent his summers playing lacrosse in Ottawa and Toronto and was "perhaps the highest-paid man"[6] in that sport. He preferred to be in Renfrew for the winter, where, recognized by all as Stimmy, he was a well-known fixture.

All the Creamery Kings were, as the new year evolved. Heads turned whenever they walked, invariably as a group, along the streets of Renfrew. Hundreds sought out the practice times for the team and made their way to the rink, entering much as they would a church, to see these hockey Messiahs who would lead Renfrew to the promised Stanley Cup. All levels of Renfrew society were infected:

*The professional hockey players are already well-known personally to railbirds at the rink. Many other  citizens saw them for the first time when they occupied  a complimentary box at the O'Brien Opera House on  Friday night last. And the general comment was that  they were a fine looking lot of men.*[7]

During that first week in January, the Galt hockey team played Ottawa in a Stanley Cup challenge. It represented an opportunity for Renfrew to scout Ottawa. Even more so, it offered M.J. the opportunity to show off his Valley boys in front of the Ottawa fans, embarrassing the home-town club in the process. The Ottawa *Citizen* carried the report under the headline: "Hostile Hockeyists Invade City."[8]

*. . . The Renfrew delegation was headed by Ambrose O'Brien and George Barnet. All the players except Herb Jordan were there. Jordan had taken a new position in Renfrew and was too industrious to leave. Members of  the team attended a theatre party as guests of Billy O'Brien and sat together at the match last evening. Conspicuous in the party was Fred Taylor who laughed when told of reports that he was going to play with Ottawa. Fred Taylor declared that he has appointed Lester Patrick as his financial advisor. Patrick stuck to the Listowel Cyclone yesterday, fearing, evidently, that Bruce Stuart or Peter Green might attempt to kidnap him.*[9]

The reporter might have been writing tongue in cheek but it was obvious that Renfrew wasn't taking any chances. They didn't want Taylor changing his mind again. Some of the Ottawa executive were still smarting from the way they felt they were used. They were calling for the club to seek a court injunction to prohibit Taylor from playing with anyone but Ottawa. Club vice-president, LLewellyn Bate, eventually won out, however. Taylor had participated in more practices with

Renfrew than he had with Ottawa "thus earning the money which he accepted early in the week."[10]

On the last day of 1909, the employees of the railroad lands branch of the Department of the Interior, convinced now that Taylor was leaving them, joined together to give him a going-away gift. Taylor was to say in later years that he simply took a "leave of absence,"[11] but certainly the department and its members considered it permanent. Every employee was there to watch Stanley Turnbull present a "magnificent grip . . . his initials inscribed."[12] There had been gossip that Taylor had not been liked within the department because of the methods used to obtain his position, but none of this was evident on that Friday afternoon at the touching ceremony. Everyone applauded enthusiastically. It seemed obvious, however, that there was just as much, if not more, concern about Taylor leaving the hockey team as there was about his going from the department as everyone expressed the hope, "Fred would once again wear the Ottawa colours, but, they wished him all kinds of success with Renfrew."[13] For his part, the "Listowel boy stated that he will always keep and cherish the gift as a remembrance of his pleasant days in the Interior Department."[14]

And the Ottawa players? Like any, they were sad to see their team-mate leave; it would adversely affect the club and their chances of repeating as Stanley Cup champions, but they were not about to let him know that. They cheerfully "informed Taylor that they will invite him to their Stanley Cup banquet in the Spring."[15] Taylor good-naturedly countered by "declaring that the banquet will take place at M.J. O'Brien's new hotel in Renfrew."[16] Behind all the banter, of course, was the realization that the season was about to begin and the pay-cheques flow, and because of Taylor, the Patricks and the Renfrew millionaires, everybody's envelope would be much larger this year! And thank goodness for that! The coverage of the recent Montreal Shamrocks/All Montreal game reinforced the notion to the players that they had to get it while they could. There was no players' association, medical plan or hospital coverage, artificial ice or climate-controlled buildings. In Montreal, a number of players ended up with bruises from the "bitterly cold weather (making) the sheet of ice a trifle too keen for some of the players' skates. There were many tumbles."[17] Some of the players suffered from frost-bite, "Marks of All Montreal, being the chief sufferer with his left foot frozen."[18]

Those thoughts, however, were far removed from the Renfrew players as they continued their social whirl with the Cyclone in Renfrew. Indeed, when the Renfrew ladies hockey team was challenged by their Pembroke counterpart, it was arranged to have Fred Taylor and Lester Patrick officiate. Not only that, each side was given nicknames: the Cyclones and the Whirlwinds. The reporter from the Pembroke *Observer* was ecstatic, indeed awed by the appearance of the two superstars, about whom so much had been written and so few, away from the league circuit, would have the opportunity to see. It was obvious that their reputation as the new breed of admired professional hockey players had preceded them. Far from being critical and spiteful, the reporter was absolutely enthralled. The two were modest and made no attempt to upstage the ladies. And yet, they *could not fail to win the wondering admiration of all as in the discharge of their duties, they threaded their way among the players, skating now forward, now backward, as occasion demanded, with unvarying skill and celerity, and never by chance, colliding, or in the slightest degree, interfering with any of the players. As one watched these evidently unconscious displays of skill, it did not appear at all astonishing that these  men should earn enormous remuneration for their services during the short hockey season.*[19]

The ladies were not forgotten in the reporter's rush to gush over the two luminaries. His description, "Ladies Hockey Match A Brilliant Function," was effervescent:

*Under the brilliant lights of the rink, the red and  white uniforms flashing backward and forward, hither  and thither, now mingling, massing, wheeling and  scattering as they produced kaleidoscopic effects, the  pictures presented were colourful, brilliant, and  vibrant with shimmering animation.*[20]

Effusive language aside, there was no doubt that the professionals were being celebrated throughout Renfrew and the Valley. One particular twelve-year-old, Charlotte Whitton, Lottie to her friends, was particularly enthralled. She attended virtually every practice, got to know the players by name and became an unofficial adoptee of the team. Indeed, on her fourteenth birthday the team and Uncle Imjay arranged to have her as the guest of honour, sitting her in a special distinguished box in back of the bench. She was later to reflect that the players spent much time with the youth of Renfrew, passing on many hockey tips or simply conversing with them. Many of the townspeople made it a point to pass by the *Mercury* offices where, particularly on a sunny day, the players could be seen sitting in the warmth "like graven images."[21]

Even though the Patricks and Taylor were non-drinkers, some felt that, at times, the players drank too much. Indeed, Renfrew was about to vote upon doing away with alcoholic beverages. Some felt that it had become too large a problem and should be stopped. The temperance advocates won out. Liquor was banned. The Ottawa *Citizen* couldn't resist:

*Horrors! Could you picture the Stanley Cup feeling at  home in a dry town? Good hockey players and temperance  advocates seldom associate. Good thing the Renfrew  magnates got their team together before election day!*[22]

It was becoming apparent, even in Ottawa, that there seemed to be more news and information being generated about the NHA than there was about the CHL. Renfrew was gaining a huge following at the expense of the Ottawa club, which didn't seem to be helping its own situation. When the Stanley Cup holders refused to allow  season-ticket holders to purchase their seats for the Stanley Cup series with Galt, angry letters to the editor attacked the club's haughtiness. Writers, many anonymous, were also taking the "occasion to tell the Ottawas that they're in the wrong league and that their staunchest followers will refuse to patronize them in the future."[23]

The aura surrounding Renfrew continued to glow when court proceedings between the Montreal Nationals and Canadiens were made public. The two teams, in rival leagues, each vying for the French Canadian following, were seeking to have the courts decide who would have the services of Didier Pitre. He eventually was declared the property of the Canadiens, but the significant item of information, which fed the evergrowing Renfrew mythology, was the news that the entire salary budget of the Nationals was four thousand, five-hundred and thirty dollars,[24] less than the two Patricks were earning with Renfrew and, setting tongues wagging even more, less than the Cyclone alone was reaping!

Excitement continued to mount, building to a peak. Hockey talk was everywhere as the beginning of the season moved ever closer. It wasn't so much that Ottawa supporters weren't interested in their team, there just seemed to be more excitement about the Renfrew bunch. Oh, there was still the odd shot taken by the Ottawa newspapers. They were likely to refer to the Valley townspeople as pirates but even that connotation elicited a swashbuckling image of excitement. When the Ottawa firm of Messrs Hurd and Company shipped the Renfrew pirates their sweaters, they were described as, "about the nicest that have been made up for some time. The colour scheme, although vivid, does not really rival the Ottawa sweaters for loudness, the Renfrew Magnates sticking to the old design which has made the team famous."[25] The sweaters were described as having "red shoulders with a white body. An old English "R" will complete the sweater.". . . Red stockings with white stripes in the middle, made up the outfit. . . coat sweaters were also "purchased by the millionaires, the design being very nifty."[26]

The Ottawa firm, "on account of the importance attached to the order,"[27] was able to get the sweaters ready in time for the opening game against Cobalt on January 12. It was an indication that even the hockey suppliers were convinced that the NHA was uppermost in the public's mind and more importantly from their perspective, it was here to stay. The company issued a booklet containing the entire list of games in the Canadian National, Interprovincial and City Leagues.

It was the Renfrew team, however, which was capturing everybody's imagination. The *Journal* mused, "it would take much more than the capacity of the Renfrew rink to accommodate the crowd which is desirous of seeing"[28] the players in action.

As the opening game approached, so too did the excitement. It was certain that the *Journal* was right. The rink would not be big enough. In fact, "some dollar seats were sold for as high as four dollars," a situation causing the newspaper to call the town "hockey mad."[29] The two thousand or so spectators were partisanly in favour of the home side. They completely drowned out the few who had journeyed from the silver mines in the northland that was Cobalt. Indeed, it was looked upon by some as a type of house-league game. After all, Tommy Hare and his Cobalt group were somewhat supported by M.J. and his silver-mine operations.

The Ottawa *Citizen*, eager to capitalize on all the excitement, announced grand plans for the game. Not only would it send reporter Tommy Gorman to catch the "timberwolf special," arriving from Ottawa in time to watch the game, returning on the 5 am from Renfrew, it also decided to "supply a first class bulletin service in both the Ottawa Amateur Athletic Club and the YMCA."[30] Gorman's task was to write up the game for the paper's readers but, as well, flash the news of each score to Ottawa on the special wire, leased for the occasion. The scores were to be posted on the bulletin-boards where they would be "a big hit with the crowds who no doubt would be on hand to hear tonight's hockey returns from Renfrew."[31]

When the Renfrew seven took to the ice that night of January 12, the noise of expectation was deafening. The Patricks, Taylor, Lindsay, Rowe, Jordan, and Arnprior native Jack

Fraser were the centre of attention. Fraser, who had previously played in Manitoba, had been called upon in order to replace Gilmour. Eyes were upon him to see if he could keep up with his storied team-mates. The eyes soon changed focus. Cobalt's team showed that they would be no push-overs. They played with the certainty that comes from having played a couple of games together and skated away with an 11-9 victory.

The stunning loss was such a surprise that the Ottawa *Citizen* devoted a half-page to the game, complete with photographs. A neighbouring Valley-town newspaper dubbed the Renfrew team Gold Bricks. The *Mercury* story was headed: "Alas! Poor Renfrew."[32] Throughout the town, the next morning, wherever people gathered, the discussion turned to hockey. "Wasn't it a shame?" was the underlying theme. But almost in the same breath, the conversation turned to the dashes of Lester Patrick, the spectacular rushes of Taylor, his unpredictability and the lack of his team-mates' familiarity with his style of play in game conditions; the heavy emphasis that Renfrew had placed on the offensive aspects of the game, preferring to outscore the opposition; and the results of being caught up ice allowing Cobalt to pour in, almost at will, on poor Bert Lindsay who was left to fend for himself. Jordan showed that he could play, scoring three goals and Fraser, the Arnprior boy, was a pleasant surprise, but would the Creamery Kings seek improvement in that position? And wasn't that some check thrown on Patrick by Smaill early in the game?

Indeed, the Montreal *Gazette* offered an interesting insight into the match. Very early in the contest, Cobalt's Walter Smaill set the tempo of what could be expected by Renfrew when he collided heavily with Frank Patrick. Oh, it wasn't dirty, mind you, but it was rambunctious with heavy emphasis on the *ram*. Patrick was sent crashing to the ground, unconscious for a few moments. He struggled to his feet, blood trickling from a broken nose. Gamely, he continued. But he was "never himself during the (rest of the) game."[33] It was obvious that the Cobalt strategy was to hit Renfrew early and often, to slow them down, to help them lose their concentration. It was a strategy as old as the game itself. . . and it worked. The Renfrew stars were extinguished and brought back down to earth.

There was very little rancour in the town, no sense of betrayal. The people had seen enough to know that they had the makings of a championship team. With only a twelve-game season, however, there was very little time to develop slowly. The *Journal* dissected the game and offered a variety of explanatory reasons for the outcome: it was Renfrew's first game. Cobalt had already played two and were game-wise. The rink was too small; it hindered the free-wheeling style of Taylor. There were too many offsides by the home team but once they became used to playing with each other, the situation would rectify itself.

Indeed, the offsides were so irritating, plentiful and frustrating that Taylor muttered to referee Fred Lake, "Ok, Fred, give us some sort of chance." Taylor was "sent to the fence for three minutes."[34] In fact, Renfrew had eighteen minutes in penalties. Not only were they playing six versus seven much of the time, their offensive energy was being expended chasing the puck in a defensive role. In an effort to hide Frank Patrick, who, because of his broken nose, was unable to play his defensive position, the team moved him to one of the wings and put Fraser at the other, his opposite one.[35]

All of the above were offered as explanations for the defeat of the all-stars. Lester Patrick had yet another one, perhaps the most telling: "Unfortunately, the opening of the season interfered with our Renfrew social activities. We couldn't please the O'Briens in the drawing-room and the arena too."[36] Patrick sought out O'Brien and then the players. He had a simple request: place the emphasis more on hockey and less on extra-curricular social activities.

Time wasn't on the side of the Renfrew team. There couldn't be too many changes made, in spite of the shortcomings one might have noticed. The next game was on January 15, in

Montreal, against the Wanderers. Travel would take up the better part of the day; there was little opportunity to step up the tempo in practice. With the long-term solutions difficult to speed up, the O'Briens reverted to standard practice, for them - they tried to buy a solution. Edmonton was in Ottawa preparing to challenge for the Cup. Its players were well-known to Patrick. The O'Briens decided to make a pitch for Hay Miller, the outstanding player of the western team. If Miller would join Renfrew for the one game, Saturday night, against the Wanderers, Renfrew would play him on the wing where he was sorely needed. In return, Renfrew would provide an all-expenses-paid trip to the game in Montreal for his team-mates to watch the game and pay Miller the sum of one thousand dollars! It was an astonishing offer, the equivalent of twelve thousand dollars for the season! Miller did not accept: he had given his word to Edmonton that he would be fully ready to play the Stanley Cup series with them and that included being at the rink in Ottawa on Saturday night in order to scout the Stanley Cup holders with his team-mates.

As far as the Ottawa *Journal* was concerned, the proposition was mind-boggling. "Doping out that salary, mathematically, brings out some surprising figures. Miller could not have played more than sixty minutes. At that salary, his services were worth more than sixteen dollars and sixty cents a minute. Or finer still, about one quarter, two bits, for every second!"[37]

When the Renfrews took to the ice against Montreal, their line-up was intact from the first game. Their reputation had preceded them. The Jubilee arena was jammed "three thousand people crowding the rink, though hundreds could not get in."[38] The earlier controversy about the arena and the Jubilee rink seemed to be on the reporter's mind: "Had the game been at a better rink," he wrote, "probably five thousand would have attended."[39] The Wanderers jumped into an early 4-0 lead after twenty minutes. Renfrew then seemed to find itself. While the score ended in a 7-2 victory for Montreal, "the contest was marked by fast spectacular hockey. . . Renfrew came back hard and fought so well that the issue was always doubtful."[40]

True! None of the media seemed down on the team, nor did the fans feel that they were cheated out of seeing something that they were expecting to see. In fact, they seemed genuinely ecstatic that their Wanderers had beaten such an all-star collection. But the players were grim. The players had played two games and had lost two! All seemed hopeless. And then, an announcement was made that threw everybody into a tizzy. Ottawa and the Shamrocks were joining the NHA!

*Frank Cosentino*

# Chapter Five

*Reality*

As far as Charlotte Whitton was concerned, M.J. O'Brien's goal in hockey was not only to win the Stanley Cup but "to rub Ottawa's nose in it."[1] Now that he had Ottawa by the neck, there was no way he was going to let go, to let them wriggle loose. Ottawa was on the run; there would be no concessions.

From every point of view, whether it was quality of play, attendance, publicity, whatever, the National Hockey Association was outgaining the Canadian. The latter had only one major asset - the Stanley Cup went to the winner! That was the one thing that O'Brien and the rest of his fellow owners wanted and the way to get it was to allow Ottawa to enter the National Hockey Association.

There was bluffing on both sides. Ottawa wanted in; the NHA wanted the right to compete for the Cup. The National owners were convinced that Ottawa wanted in more; they were adamant - there would be no concessions.

When the meeting commenced at Ottawa's Windsor Hotel, the president of the NHA, Mike Doheny of Renfrew, was absent. Weldy Young, the former member of the Dawson City Stanley Cup challengers of 1905, was in the chair representing Haileybury. Perhaps Young had something to prove too. His team was blasted by the Silver Seven in the second game by a 23-2 score, the match in which the legendary one-eyed Frank McGee scored his record fourteen goals!

Ambrose O'Brien was also present in his capacity as secretary of the association. In an earlier caucus of the NHA clubs, it had been decided that not all members of the CHA would be accepted. That would allow them to hold the balance of power in any vote. No, applications would be called for and discussed individually.

The formal part of the meeting began at 4 pm in room thirty-five. It lasted until 9 pm. There had already been discussion within the NHA group as to what would happen if Ottawa and the Shamrocks chose to apply. They would be "favourably considered."[2] Quebec and the All Montreals were to be turned down; the Montreal Nationals would be given a proposal. Some doubted that Ottawa would humble itself to request admission. Rather than debate the possibility, Ottawa president D'arcy McGee was invited to address the meeting. He suggested that the two leagues amalgamate. The NHA teams said no. McGee said that Ottawa would consider joining the NHA, if Fred Taylor were given back to them. Again, the answer was no. Of course, discussion did not stop there. It went on and on, but, no matter what arguments were advanced by Ottawa, the answer was always the same - no!

In the end, Ottawa and the Shamrocks were accepted as members of the National Hockey Association. The seven teams would play a twelve-game schedule, beginning with the games on January 15; the Cobalt/Haileybury match on March 15 would be the last. The team with the most points at the end of the twelve games would be the Stanley Cup champion.

At first, it appeared that Renfrew would object to the beginning date. On further examination, however, there appeared to be more pluses than minuses in the arrangement. Renfrew would only have one loss instead of two; it would also have a twelve-game schedule instead of eight and that meant two more home games. It also meant that Ottawa with three overwhelming victories, 14-4, 15-5, and 15-3, would only count their last, the 15-3 score over the Shamrocks. The Wanderers would also only count one of their two, the 7-2 win over Renfrew. But there was no question that the biggest inducement of all was that Ottawa had been humbled. The Stanley Cup was in sight!

The fall-out of the meeting continued long after the nine o'clock adjournment. The Canadian Hockey Association was disbanded. Their players became available to other clubs. Haileybury picked up Paddy Moran and Art Ross from the All Montreals. The Quebec franchise folded. The Montreal Nationals were given the opportunity to purchase the Canadiens franchise. The Nationals owners were much better heeled than the Canadiens group but the old site problems, the arena versus the Jubilee, were too great. The Nationals were bound to the arena and its larger capacity; the Canadiens had a three-year contract with the Jubilee. It was an impossible situation and the Nationals executive were furious. They probably would have joined the NHA when it was first formed; they had the opportunity and were the group's first choice, but they chose to align themselves with Ottawa and the Shamrocks in the CHA. Now, they were placed in this impossible situation. Along with All Montreal and Quebec, they dropped out of existence, wiser in the ways of the hockey world, but poorer for it.

In a compromise move, Emmett Quinn of the former CHA and James McCafferty of the NHA were appointed co-presidents of the new group and Lunny and McGee were added to the executive. It was now a seven-team group: Ottawa, the Shamrocks, the Wanderers, the Canadiens, Cobalt, Haileybury, and of course, Renfrew. There was no question that it would provide the best hockey in the country. Renfrew had eleven games remaining to demonstrate that the Creamery Kings were the *crème de la crème* - and the proud holders of the Stanley Cup.

But there was little time to gloat over the turn of events. Renfrew's next contest was January 19 with the Montreal Canadiens led by Didier Pitre and Newsy Lalonde. Over one thousand fans watched in glee as the home-town Creamery Kings recorded their first victory, 9-4. Prominent among the spectators was Fred Whitcroft, from Edmonton, "who declared Taylor to be the greatest player he had ever seen."[3]

It was an overdue result as far as many were concerned. The fans "went into a frenzy as the Red and White players forged away ahead."[4] It was the first evidence their followers had had that Renfrew could play as a team. Or as the *Mercury* phrased it in its attribution of the victory: "the desire of each of the stars to shine individually, becoming less prominent."[5] But even so, the talk around town was about the fight which had broken out between Frank Patrick and Newsy Lalonde. Both Patricks had been involved with the combative Lalonde. Lester, as Captain, and supporter of Frank, found himself constantly involved with the fiery Frenchman. Three times, they were sent off together:

*the rival captains slashing at each other with their fists and sticks on several occasions. In the second half, Patrick cut Lalonde's head open with a swing of his stick, and as soon as the Renfrew leader got back on the ice, Lalonde caught him with a wicked cross check that sent the famous rover into the air as if shot from a cannon.*[6]

Perhaps smarting from the attack by Smaill in the first home game, Frank Patrick was aware that he would again be the subject of heavy checking. Like many hockey players, he had been told that unless he stood up to it every time, the heavy hitting would follow him for the rest of his career - and his big brother wouldn't be there to protect him forever. The normally quiet Patrick played an aggressive game, initiating many hits. Lalonde took exception to one particularly hard check. He was ready to fight at any time and he didn't appreciate someone trying to run over him. He turned and butt-ended Patrick, high on the neck. A gash was opened behind Patrick's ear. Blood started to flow. The fans were on their feet shouting obscenities at the Canadiens' star.

Frank Patrick was knocked off balance, stunned. He couldn't go down again! Not for the second consecutive game! He wheeled and delivered a similar blow to Lalonde's head, knocking him down. Both players lay on the ice, holding their heads. Attendants administered to them while the crowd vented its anger against Lalonde and the rest of his team-mates, who wisely chose to leave the ice for the safety of the dressing-room until the crowd's emotions cooled.

The incident seemed to ignite the home side; the Canadiens' fire seemed extinguished. And Patrick and Lalonde? Far from carrying on their feud, they joined each other after the game, returning to Patrick's boarding-house for a post-game snack and coffee. The incident was forgotten, a friendship forged - a friendship which was to pay dividends later on.

Hockey was again the topic of conversation in town. "The brilliant rushes of Taylor, the Patricks and those visitors who folded,"[7] were on everybody's lips. Almost buried, was the news that Ottawa had once again defended its Stanley Cup championship with a victory over Edmonton in the two-game series, 8-4 on January 18, and 13-7 on January 20. Indeed, that news might have remained buried except for two reasons. Firstly, by winning, Ottawa guaranteed that the trophy would remain in the hands of the winner of the newly expanded NHA. Secondly, and just as importantly, was the news that the millionaires were at it again. Both Hay Millar and Fred Whitcroft signed on with the O'Brien team, prior to its game with the Montreal Shamrocks. Whitcroft, "a star of the first water,"[8] whose "work was one of the big sensations"[9] in the recently concluded series, and Millar, whose reputation suffered somewhat, "a lack of condition being his excuse,"[10] were "understood to be getting the same kind of salary that tempted Fred Taylor to leave Ottawa and Lester Patrick to forsake Nelson."[11]

*The Globe* fixed their contracts at two thousand dollars for the remaining ten games of the season. The signings meant that Renfrew would release a young maritimer, Chester Gregory, whom they had been grooming, and Jack Fraser, the Arnprior native. Both would be kept around in the event of an emergency. Such was the world of professional hockey. Millar and Whitcroft had much better credentials and could be what was needed to bring the Stanley Cup to Renfrew.

Indeed the victory, followed by the news of two more stars joining the team, caused much serious discussion throughout the town and elsewhere where hockey followers gathered, and that seemed to be just about everywhere! The consensus seemed to be that while Renfrew had the best players to be found anywhere, they would have to learn to play as a team or they would not gain their prize, the Stanley Cup. They would also have to learn to handle the approach of the opposition. It was obvious that the Millionaires, as they were beginning to be called, would have to learn to cope with the tactic of being run at by other teams. Rightly or wrongly, other association members were convinced that they had to hit and intimidate the high-flying Renfrew team to throw them off their game, to make them think about the other team's men rather than the puck. Renfrew needed good, hard, fast ice and room to roam. The last half of the Canadiens' game demonstrated that. The next match, January 22, against the Montreal Shamrocks, would reinforce it. The Irish team had played only one game, against Ottawa, in the old Canadian Association. The fast-skating Stanley Cup champions had moved through and around the Montrealers at will, outscoring them 15-3. Bad Joe Hall had been neutralized, unable to hit what he couldn't catch.

Renfrew had no such luck. The weather turned warm; the ice was slushy. Pools of water were everywhere. Players who were knocked down were drenched, slowed down by the weight of their sopping uniforms when they arose and joined the play. It was perfect weather for the slower Shamrocks, delivering the collection of all-stars right into their hands; no, into their sites, like sitting ducks! Through the first half, tempers seemed ready to explode. Bad Joe was continually running at the Patricks. The Cyclone was being lined up constantly - but he had the deftness to escape and in the process, cause the charger to look foolish:

*Always, he kept an opponent guessing. He loved to race ahead and then suddenly double back with the puck. This exasperated the enemy but the coolness of it provoked thunderous cheers from the fans. This is not a play that scores, as a rule, but it is a joy to watch and every creature in the grandstand has this in mind.*[12]

By half-time it was obvious that the slow ice and the chippy play of the Shamrocks were working. Renfrew had been held scoreless; the Shamrocks had scored once.

With the start of the second half, the Shamrock strategy continued. The chippiness turned to nastiness. Renfrew couldn't be seen to back down. A stick-swinging duel was the ominous sign that the game was deteriorating. Montreal player Barney Holden, frustrated by the you-can't-hit-what-you-can't-catch, stop-and-go tactics of Taylor, swung his stick in the direction of the Cyclone's head. Taylor retaliated in kind and connected. Holden's nose was bloodied. He rushed Taylor. Lester Patrick led the Renfrew players to their team-mate's defense. The Shamrocks moved in to help Holden. Pushing, shoving, stick swinging and splashes of water fuelled the altercation. Joe Hall moved into the fray, circling until he paired up with Frank Patrick. Again, the younger of the two brothers had been the subject of much stick and body-checking during the night. But he had also fought back, too hard insisted Hall, who said that he had been cross-checked by Patrick without a penalty being called.

 When the Judge of Play, Rod Kennedy, finally restored order it was obvious that emotions were still running high. Only a slight spark was needed to rekindle yet another explosion. It came with fifteen minutes left in the second half. Hall was continually frustrated in his attempts to corner Frank Patrick. The latter was retaliating and Bad Joe had already been bloodied from one exchange. By now Hall was furious and after one more collision with Patrick, where Hall was knocked down, he got up and:

*went splashing up the ice after Frank who hit him again. Hall stopped in his tracks and struck back with his stick, slicing Patrick's cheek. A lively scrap ensued during which Hall received yet another gash, this time over the eye.*[13]

The "lively scrap" terminated when "Hall dropped his stick and hit Patrick who countered with a Jefferys punch."[14]

Players and officials rushed in to part the two before the fight degenerated into a free-for-all. Both players were separated and started to skate off towards the penalty box. They had each been given a two-minute penalty. Suddenly, "the crowd witnessed the extraordinary spectacle of Hall attacking Judge of Play, Rod Kennedy." It was the second time that Hall had become involved with the official. The first occurred when, during the fight with Patrick, Kennedy had held him back. When the two players fell to the ice, Hall "kicked out with his feet, one of his skates tearing a piece of Kennnedy's trousers." The act was done in the frustration of the moment; there appeared to be no deliberation about it. It was just part of the famous temper that Joe Hall had, the reason for his nickname Mean or Bad.

But the second attack on Kennedy was not so easily explained away, although an attempt was made to do so. Skating towards the timer's bench to serve his penalty, his face bloodied from a cut on his forehead, Hall lunged at Kennedy "viciously with his fist,"[15] and "gave him a stinging blow in the face."[16] However, to the surprise of all, the Judge of Play "retaliated by knocking Hall down with a blow which closed his two eyes and cut his face."[17]

By now, the players had paired off. "Don Smith held Frank's brother Lester, pinned against the boards, as Hall, screaming epithets, was finally dragged to the dressing-room, and was put out of play for the balance of the match. He had played dirty all through it and his attacks on Patrick and Kennedy were inexcusable. Hall deserved more punishment than he received."[18]

It was a spectacle that nobody relished but everyone understood its happening with the unpredictable Bad Joe Hall in the line-up. He had a reputation as a dirty player, a reputation that many of his team-mates said was overrated. Much of his combativeness was due to his being forced to stand up to other toughs wanting to test themselves against the man considered to be the toughest in hockey. It wasn't the only time that Hall would take on an official. Later, as a member of the Quebec Bulldogs, he was fined and suspended for his attack on referee Tom Melville. He and Newsy Lalonde, himself one of the most combative players in the National, were to have many bitter battles during their careers until they declared a truce. Hall was later to become a member of the Montreal Canadiens. In the fifth game of the Stanley Cup series against Seattle in 1919, he took sick with the flu and died a few days later in a Seattle hospital. The series, hard hit by the influenza outbreak, was never finished.

Back at the Jubilee rink, however, the crowd sat in stunned disbelief, having expended enough energy for two games while emotionally involving themselves in the continuing battles throughout the match. They watched as Judge of Play Kennedy skated to the timer's bench to report that Frank Patrick was being assessed a two-minute penalty and Hall was out for the rest of the evening. The Shamrocks were still leading by a 1-0 score. With the expiration of Patrick's penalty, Renfrew would have a one-man advantage for fifteen minutes.

For the next two minutes, with the teams playing six a side, Renfrew assumed a conservative style, not wanting to be caught up ice as they pressed to tie the score. They seemed content to wait until they had the man advantage. After the two minutes were up, Frank Patrick returned to the ice. Now

Renfrew opened it up, hoping that the rapidly deteriorating conditions wouldn't equalize their extra-man advantage. Passing was becoming difficult. Huge sprays of water were sent into the air with each movement of the sticks upon the ice. With only a few minutes left before the end of time, Frank Patrick, his adrenalin still flowing from the earlier events, scored the tying goal. Renfrew seemed content to play for the tie in regulation time knowing that, with the brief intermission, the ice would be cleared of the excess water. They could then go on the attack with their man advantage under better conditions.

Referee Tom Hodge blew his whistle to signal the beginning of the overtime period. "The Irish wanted to put a new man out in the place of Hall whose optics were closed as a result of meeting Kennedy's fist."[19] Renfrew objected: Hall had been thrown out for the duration of the contest; the contest was still being played. Neither Hall nor a substitute should be allowed to play.

A split developed between the officials. Referee Tom Hodge was in favour of allowing Hall to return. He cited as a precedent a Stanley Cup game in 1903. Then, Winnipeg's Kean had been thrown out for breaking Gardner's, of Montreal, collar-bone. When the game ended in a tie, Winnipeg proposed to return Kean to the ice for the overtime; Montreal did not object. "Pshaw," or words to that effect - Renfrew did object! And they were backed by Judge of Play Kennedy. "The rag-chewing and wrangling went on for nearly three quarters of an hour while the audience waited macawberlike for something to turn up."[20] Strangely enough, the league had not designed rules to cover the situation, one the Toronto *Globe* described as "absurd."[21]

Gradually, the crowd began to filter out of the rink, unaware of what the final verdict would be but not wanting to stay around all night to find out. Again, the whistle was blown to bring both teams to centre ice to begin the overtime session. The two teams refused to leave their respective dressing-rooms. More people left. Finally, after another wait of close to an hour, the game was called; a decision was made to replay it at a later date.

In spite of everything, the game was summarized as:

*a corker, with both teams evenly matched, perhaps because of the slushy ice with great pools of water in places. These conditions told against the teamwork and fast play as players frequently overskated the puck. It was fast in spite of the poor conditions of the ice. Right from the drop of a hat, they went at it hammer and tongs. The game was rough all through. Cross-checking, slashing, tripping and hard blows were given and taken as a matter of course. In a short time, the players got beyond the control of the referees and the game resembled a donneybrook fair more than a decent respectable hockey match.*[22]

In the aftermath of the game, tempers had cooled because of the long wait. The uniforms, wet from the ice conditions and the perspiration, had been removed and hung. Neither team was all that anxious to continue. It was a sheepish Joe Hall who approached Rod Kennedy, "shook his hand, apologized for the swollen eye and explained that with blood in both of his eyes, he hadn't known who he was hitting."[23] The apology was accepted but throughout the league and wherever hockey players gathered, another story about Bad Joe Hall was added to the growing number, and Kennedy would always be known as the official who decked Joe Hall.

The Renfrew executive were adamant that the issue would not end there. After all, they had seen too many opposing teams begin to run at their team in an effort to intimidate and throw them off their game. There was to be a rematch of the two teams within the week in Renfrew. The club was determined that Joe Hall would be suspended.

Meanwhile, the Millionaires made their way to Ottawa where they would change trains. To the casual observer, they appeared to have returned from a combat zone, "most of the men bearing a host of scars as a result of the Shamrock game."[24] The newly arrived Fred Whitcroft had lost a tooth; Lester Patrick's face "had a very nasty gash above the left side";[25] Frank Patrick's face was marked up as was Bobby Rowe's. "Most of the players can thank Hall for their injuries and all are hoping that 'Bad Joe' is not fired out of the league before the Shamrocks go to Renfrew Friday night."[26]

Whether Renfrew wanted revenge in the rematch, feeling more confident in their home environment, or whether they simply did not want to see a hockey player lose his opportunity to earn a salary, is not known. But certainly the Renfrew executive felt differently. They called for a meeting of the National Hockey Association to discuss the situation. Three teams were needed to call an emergency session. Interestingly the three were Renfrew, Haileybury and the Canadiens, all clubs in which O'Brien had some stake. The result was that Joe Hall was to be suspended for two games, against Renfrew and the Canadiens, with his case to be further discussed at another meeting to be called on February 2.

There was a decidedly relaxed atmosphere about the Millionaires that week prior to the January 28 rematch with the Shamrocks. Probably the removal of Hall had something to do with it. Other Montreal players were less likely to be as belligerent, knowing that Hall would not be on the ice to bail them out. Players lingered a little longer, in the dressing-room or at the café, after practice. It was an opportunity to get to know one another, to tell a few stories, each outdoing the other. One evening, when Fred Whitcroft began to narrate his baseball exploits with the Young Liberals team in Edmonton (a team coached by the well-known Deacon White who would later become coach of the Edmonton Eskimos, Grey Cup finalists of 1921), he emphasized his hitting prowess. He batted .700, superb in any league in the 1908 season. These were the fish stories, and this was too good an opportunity to pass up and let slip by. Fred Taylor, with a straight face and a look of feigned disgust, peered up from tying his skates. He could remember the time, he said, when his team was three runs behind and men were on second and third. He lashed a hit to deep centre field and ran the bases so fast that he beat both his team-mates to home plate!

Meanwhile, the Renfrew public, preparing itself for the return game, was somewhat disappointed when Mean Joe's suspension was announced. They wanted to see this legendary bad boy. News of Hall's antics had made the rounds for years, his meanness increasing with each telling of a tale. The townspeople were all set to prepare a hot reception. A full house was virtually guaranteed, in spite of what some considered to be exorbitant prices.

Throughout the league, there had been much discussion about the seating prices. Salaries had certainly escalated tremendously, thanks to O'Brien and his newly created Millionaires. Renfrew was charging one dollar for a front-row seat, seventy-five cents for a second-row and fifty cents for general admission. Even with those prices, there was little guarantee that the club would support itself. Players' salaries were simply too high. In Montreal, the new Jubilee rink was thought to have reasonable prices. General admission was only thirty-five cents; reserved cost seventy-five cents and one dollar. If someone wanted a reserved box, they would have to pay two dollars. Ottawa's prices were considered to be even better yet, perhaps because of the large number of seats they had in their Laurier Street arena. Twenty-five cents could buy standing room; a reserved seat could be bought for fifty cents. The highest prices were in the northland, in Cobalt and Haileybury, "up in the silver country, (where) they sometimes get as much as ten dollars for a seat."[27] Supply and demand had much to do with the prices. If one were to purchase season-tickets, the prices would be constant but, for the ones sold the night of the game, there was always some discussion as to whether or not to raise the prices.

If the Renfrew fans were expecting fireworks at the Shamrock game, they were disappointed. A full house was there, expecting to see a continuation of the rough play of last week.

The ice was "hard and as keen as steel,"[28] and for the first ten minutes, the play was fast and furiously paced. The Shamrocks were all over the ice, having got the jump on the home side; it was only the sparkling goal-tending of Bert Lindsay, who made a series of sensational saves, which kept Renfrew in the game. From that time on, however, "the match was far from exciting and at times, play lagged. . . Renfrew did not have to overexert themselves to win."[29] The final score was Renfrew, 10, Shamrocks, 2. Perhaps it was the expectation of tempers flaring which, not having materialized, made the game appear slower than usual. Certainly, there were plenty of moments to cherish: the play of Lindsay, the first appearance before the home fans of the Edmonton duo of Millar and Whitcroft - they were said to have added "both speed and brains to the Renfrew line-up."[30] Taylor seemed to be concentrating more on his defensive game but the Patricks, always crowd favourites, were keyed up for the game, they always seemed to be. And maybe they wanted a little revenge for the previous meeting; they contributed six of the ten goals!

Although Renfrew fans and players were pointing to the Ottawa game of February 12, the rough play of the opposition helped them to keep their focus on one game at a time. There were no soft touches. The mighty Wanderers had been surprised by Haileybury, losing by a 4-2 score. While Ottawa seemed to be having no trouble with any of the teams, the general feeling was that they had yet to be tested, as they would be on February 12.

The Haileybury victory over the Wanderers had done much for the northerners. Certainly, the play of Art Ross had turned them into contenders. When the Montreal team, with its well-earned reputation, appeared in the mining town for the January 22 game, the fans were unsure of the local team's chances and were unwilling to gamble in their normal fashion. When the game ended in a 4-2 victory for the miners, the word spread throughout the district. The Wanderers next game was at Cobalt and that team had already beaten the Millionaires!

Convinced that they were being given another chance to win some lucre, the silver-country residents reverted to form and wagered huge amounts of money, backing the home side and betting that the big-city boys would go down to their second consecutive defeat.

It was not to be. Perhaps it was asking too much. The Wanderers defeated the Silver Kings by an eleven-six score on January 25, the Montreal supporters happy with the win but ecstatic over the betting gains that had eluded them in Haileybury!

When Haileybury journeyed south to play in Ottawa on January 29, it gave the Renfrew team a chance to scout both opponents. Haileybury looked good; Ottawa was awesome! They scored eleven times to the visitors' four. The Senators' fans too were something else - almost an eighth man. Their noise was so great that referee Duncan Campbell was forced to use two hand bells, instead of whistles, so that the players could hear!

Meanwhile, the Bad Joe Hall saga was unfolding. Another meeting was held in Montreal on February 2. His suspension was lifted, replaced with a fine for one hundred dollars. For some players in the prior year, that would have been a full salary. Even now, there were some who were playing the full year for that sum. The motion by Renfrew was seconded by the Wanderers and was carried with little or no discussion.[31]

The Senators of Ottawa were unable to return the visit to Renfrew for that team's game with Haileybury on the 4th of February. They had their own contest with Cobalt on the 5th and were forced to take the train on the same day as the Renfrew game. But there were plenty of Ottawa fans who trained west to see Taylor perform. He still captivated fans wherever he was playing, not so much for the goals that he might score, after all he was a defenceman, but because of his effortless swooping and soaring, and his unpredictability. The Ottawa *Journal* was generous in its praise of the erstwhile Bytown star, naming him the "outstanding feature of the game." There were looks of disbelief and collective gasps of awe as he "gave a wonderful exhibition of speed and shooting. The Cyclone showed all of his old skill and his marvelous swoops down the ice with the puck sent the crowd into a frenzy."[32] Each time that he touched the puck the throng rose, as if one, in anticipation of yet another exhibition of virtuosity. On one occasion the crowd roared with delight when Taylor, behind his own net with the puck, was unchallenged by the opposition; they had withdrawn up ice to prepare for another onslaught. It was quite a sight. Lindsay was in the Renfrew net, his head as if it were on a swivel, moving from side to side, to see where Taylor would exit from behind the net. The Haileybury players, not wanting to look sillier than they already did, were content to wait for the will-o'-the-wisp to bring the puck up ice. The Renfrew fans alternated between cheering Taylor and jeering the visitors, the former hamming it up as only he could. "Fred Taylor pulled off one of his queer tricks," wrote the *Journal*, "when he posed with the puck behind his own net in the second half, the face-off being ordered when Taylor refused to skate with the rubber."[33] The Ottawa *Citizen* also described the play, calling it a "funny incident: the great and erratic Taylor, after skating round and round his net with the puck, deliberately stopped and leaned on his stick, right behind the goal. The referee blew his whistle, thinking someone was hurt, but the puck was found right at Taylor's feet. There was not a Haileybury player within twenty feet of him on either side."[34]

The whole evening was a great success. Renfrew had won the game 6-3; Taylor had put on a show and scored two goals; and Lester Patrick, "the tall Renfrew captain, was a good second to Taylor and his stick work netted three goals."[35]

At the boarding-house, long after the finish of the game, the Renfrew players were still rehashing the evening. There was some good-natured ribbing of Taylor who, once again, had been the centre of attention, overshadowing all others simply by being himself. There was much bantering back and forth as each play was re-created in detail, each giving the others the benefit of their thought processes during the action. It was like an informal team meeting. The team was coming together. It still had a long way to go but you just didn't take a group of individuals and mould them into a team overnight. At the same time, that was exactly what had to be done!

It was the type of session that the shy, reserved Frank Patrick enjoyed. He disliked talking about himself but loved to focus on others or a third party. He did a lot of thinking about hockey, was a knowledgeable student of the game, constantly looking for ways to improve it. He also had a great sense of the right thing to do, probably having learned it from his father Joe, who was a major force and influence in the Patricks' lives. After joining the others in congratulating Cyc on the game that he had played, he offered the suggestion that his game could be still improved. Taylor, with two goals and two set-ups (assists were not counted in the scoring summaries of the day), was curious. What was there that Frank had noticed that could improve his game?

Patrick noticed that whenever Taylor was in need of a rest or was being actively pursued, he simply stopped the play by flipping the puck into the crowd. Against Haileybury, he had done it five times. Taylor was flustered, asking what was the matter with that? He protested, laughingly, that it certainly was not against the rules. His team-mate agreed, but reasoned that not only were the spectators who paid good money to watch the puck on the ice cheated, but so too were the opposing players who had pursued Taylor, had put the heat on him and now were cheated of the puck that they had cornered. And there were Taylor's team-mates. They too were being cheated since they were there to help out, to receive a pass, to be part of a team, to turn the tables and place pressure on the opposition who were all bunched up around Taylor. Lastly, the younger Patrick advanced the notion that Taylor was cheating himself by simply flipping the puck over the boards. Instead, he could be developing his immense talents and skills in removing himself and the puck from such a situation.

Impressed, but unconvinced, Taylor offered the opinion that the flip was within the rules. Patrick agreed that while it was within the letter of the law, it certainly was not within the spirit. If he had his way, he said, he would propose a delay-of-game penalty for such a tactic. All heads turned now towards Patrick. The look in their eyes was obvious: Was he serious? In the middle of chasing after the Stanley Cup? With Ottawa coming up? The younger of the two Patricks saw the stares, understood what was being thought and chuckled aloud as he stated that he wouldn't propose it this season!

The post-game discussion had gone from that evening's contest itself to hockey in general and now turned to the confrontation upcoming with Ottawa, the next game that Renfrew would play. All knew of the scoring punch that the Senators had, and the proud history of their team. Known for many years as the Silver Seven they were legends in Stanley Cup play. But, at the same time, it was mentioned that one of the greatest series ever played took place in 1906 when Ottawa played the Wanderers, captained by Lester Patrick. All eyes turned to the Renfrew Captain as he began to recount that thrilling series.

Ottawa had achieved a three-year winning streak against the best teams in Canada! They had outscored all opposition one hundred and fifty-one goals to seventy-four. Their personnel had changed over the years - everybody looked at Taylor - but they always seemed to find replacements. It was March, 1906. Ottawa and Montreal had finished in a tie for the league championship. The Wanderers had defeated Ottawa by a score of 5-3 in their second meeting of the season, having lost the first one to the champions by an 8-4 count. The Wanderers had come out of the second Ottawa game crippled. Ernie Johnson had his nose broken, Billy Strachan's foot was cut and Lester Patrick was suffering from a gash over his eye, compliments of

Walter Smaill's stick - the same Mr. Smaill who had attacked Frank in the Cobalt game!

At the end of the schedule, both teams were tied in the standings with identical nine-and-one records. The ECHA decided to have a two-game, total-goals-to-count series, the winner to gain the association's championship, and the Stanley Cup. It was a bonus that club owners relished. The first game was to be played in Montreal at the arena. All season-tickets had expired. There was a great rush for seats: standing room was seventy-five cents; reserved seats were sold at one dollar; promenade locations, one dollar, fifty cents and boxes at an incredible ten dollars!

Oh, there was an outcry from the fans, to be sure, but by early morning of the day of the first game, March 14, all places were sold. Scalpers were having a field day! Patrick recounted how ten dollars was being gladly handed over for one-dollar tickets. And the game was worth it to the home-town fans! The Wanderers bottled up the Ottawa scoring machine, especially Frank McGee, and rang up four goals in the first half of play, while holding the Senators scoreless. Everybody expected that Ottawa would recover in the second half and find its scoring touch. It didn't. The Wanderers, with big Ernie Russell leading the way, Lester said (but everyone there knew that Patrick was the glue that held the team together), ended up on the long end of a 9-1 score!

It was incredible. There was sheer joy among the Wanderers and their followers. The second game was to be played in Ottawa on March 17, St. Patrick's Day and the Irish patron saint must have been looking in, said Lester. Frank chuckled. Though the family was not Catholic, they were fiercely proud of their Irish heritage. Their home in Montreal had two flags flying out front, the Union Jack and the Irish flag! During the train trip up to Ottawa, it was all that the Wanderers could do to ignore the first game, to continually remind each other that it was only half-time. Tactics became a major topic of concern. How should they best prepare themselves for the expected

Ottawa onslaught? Should they play it as a normal game? Should they play defensively and protect the eight-goal lead?

Ottawa was too proud a team with too great a history to give up. And their fans thought so too! Over five thousand crammed into every space in Dey's Arena. It was the largest crowd ever to see a game there. Earl and Lady Grey were among the spectators. Special trains from as far away as Montreal and throughout the Valley brought fans from all points, all wanting to see this wonder-team from Montreal that had made their great team appear so ordinary, and perhaps to witness the greatest come-back in the history of sport.

Ottawa replaced goalie Billie Hague with Perc LeSueur, a young goaler who had starred with Smiths Falls in an earlier Stanley Cup series. Right from the opening face-off, the strategy of both teams was obvious. Ottawa went on the offensive; Montreal would protect its lead, lifting the puck out of its zone at every opportunity. And it seemed to be working! In fact, Lester Patrick scored the first goal of the game. The round was now ten for the Wanderers, one for Ottawa. Perhaps there was a let-down by the Montrealers, but more likely it was the pride of the great team rising to the fore. At the end of the half, the game score was 3-1, Ottawa, 10-4 Montreal on the round.

Who knows what went on in their dressing-room, recalled Patrick, but at the start of the second half the Senators took to the ice playing as if they had every member who ever played with them in the past, all at the same time. They scored three goals in eighty-five seconds! It was now 10-7 on the round with all sorts of time left. Then Harry Smith went on a tear. Within the next twenty minutes, he scored three times! The series was tied! It was incredible!

Patrick had the attention of his audience. He had made his point. Ottawa was a team that had great pride, that couldn't be taken lightly. The Wanderers were clearly on the ropes and there were ten minutes remaining. The momentum was definitely with Ottawa and the five thousand spectators, screaming encouragement to the home side, on their feet as one, were conscious of it. With each goal scored by their boys, the volume of their hoarse exhortations increased. The roof was almost raised off its beams when Harry Smith scored again! What would have been his seventh of the game was waved off by the referee. Smith was offside. The goal would not count. The crowd, wild with delirious cheering, quieted down as the referee's signal was seen. The noise of the throng had made his whistle virtually ineffective.

Ottawa protested, but only mildly, aware that the play was indeed offside and referee Bob Meldrum had made the correct call, not a popular one mind you, but the correct one. It was obvious that the Wanderers' strategy had failed. The momentary debate between the referee and the Ottawa players bought the Montreal team some much needed time, some said later, for St. Patrick to do his bit.

As did Phil Esposito in the Team Canada/Soviet series of 1972, Patrick called his team-mates together in a huddle. They had to play hockey the way they knew how, the way that they had played in the first game, scoring nine goals. The Wanderers went on the attack, carrying the play into the Ottawa end. An over-anxious Harry Smith, eager to get the puck back for yet another assault on the Montreal net, was called for a penalty. It was a turning point. Lester, at the rover position, scored two goals in the last few minutes of the game. The Wanderers had won the round by 12-10! They were the Stanley Cup champions!

It was a great story. Lester tried to down play his role, preferring to laugh it off as St. Patrick's doing. He wanted to dwell more on the great tradition that Ottawa had. They could never be counted out. Renfrew would have to be prepared to play for sixty minutes against them on February 12.

# Chapter Six

## Show-down Ottawa

While Renfrew waited for the February 12 meeting with Ottawa, the Senators were in the frigid north country, winning their games with Cobalt (5-4) on February 5 and Haileybury (8-4) on February 9. These were Ottawa's eleventh and twelfth consecutive victories of the season. The team was on course for yet another Stanley Cup.

Ottawa supporters were worried about the condition of their team. There were reports of frost-bite on some of the players. Travel would certainly take its toll, in addition to the three games to be played in the one week. Renfrew, on the other hand, was well rested. The big advantage Ottawa had was that their players had been together for a longer period of time. Renfrew was still playing like a group of individuals; if they could ever turn that collection of all-stars into a team, the general feeling was that nobody could touch them.

Indeed, that must have been exactly what Ambrose O'Brien and his group were thinking too. Immediately after the game with Haileybury, Renfrew announced that Alf Smith would be retained as coach. The move would allow Lester Patrick to concentrate on playing his game without worrying about whether the others were playing as they should. More importantly, it brought an acknowledged and widely respected person into the picture in an attempt to develop team play.

Alf Smith had a good reputation in hockey circles. As a thirty-seven-year old, his playing days were over, but only recently. Probably no one knew the Senators as he did. He had been a member of the Ottawa teams when they were lauded as the Silver Seven, playing on a line with top goal scorer, Frank McGee. In addition to the capital team, he had played with Kenora and most recently with Pittsburgh in 1908/09. Throughout his career he had a penchant for rough play, seemingly a prerequisite for hockey in those days. But he was also highly skilled and adept at moving his team-mates into open ice where he would feed them passes. He had one main task with the Creamery Kings which was to mould them into a cohesive team. The Ottawa *Journal* saw that as a foregone conclusion. Preferring to call the Renfrew team by the newspaper's pet name, it opined that: "the Pirate forward line ought to be working smoother as a result of Smith's advice."[1]

As an aside, it was obvious from reports that the Renfrew team was still not widely known as the Millionaires. That would not come until after the end of the season. When the team played in New York, they were paid their salaries in cash at the end of their series. Because of the huge amounts of money that they each had in their possession, they became better known as the Millionaires.[2] Depending on who was writing about them during the course of the season, they were referred to by a variety of names. Officially, they were the Creamery Kings but just as likely Pirates, as the *Journal* preferred.

Fans in Ottawa were anxious to see Taylor return, promising him a hot time. They still had not forgiven him for his desertion to Renfrew. And the Cyclone gave them even more ammunition. A reporter had asked the Renfrew point man if he was concerned about facing his old mates? Was he worried about playing against Ottawa's strong defence and the goal-tending of Perc LeSueur? Was he intimidated by the fans? It was an innocuous type of interview; there was no need to hype the game, it was already a sell-out. But there was nothing innocuous about Taylor. His answer was duly reported - and added fuel to an already raging fire:

*Will Taylor Score? Early this week, Fred Taylor made a crack while in the* Citizen *office, Percy LeSueur being present at the time, that he would skate through the Ottawa defence backward and score a goal.*[3]

While the paper acknowledged that the hockey player stated his boast in a joking way, it also remarked that it "seems to have gotten around and been taken seriously."[4] That was an understatement. It spread like wildfire. It seemed to be on everybody's lips. Resentment was being whipped up by the brashness of the former hero of the city. The *Citizen* further reported that one "fan has posted $100. in the King Edward Hotel to bet that Taylor doesn't score in any way, shape or form . . . it can be covered on application to Mr. Peter Davis."[5]

Meanwhile, capitalizing on the intense feelings and the attendant publicity, the Ottawa executive began preparing for the expected large crowd. Season-ticket packages, even at this mid-point, were given priority. Those who purchased seats for the remainder of the season were given first call. Fans, hungry to see the game of the year, bought up all available season-ticket packages. As a result, there was such a demand for other seats that the club debated on whether or not to raise rates, from twenty-five to fifty cents, for standing room in what was called the pit. Those standing on the other side of the rink were "obliged to put up seventy-five cents."[6] Prices for the game - one dollar and fifty cents, one dollar, seventy-five cents and fifty cents for seats, plus the standing room - generated in excess of twenty-thousand dollars. "Despite their twelve-thousand-dollar-salary list, the Cup holders will be well ahead financially."[7] The anticipated sell-out crowd of close to seventy-five hundred spectators was the largest ever to see a hockey game.

It was a golden opportunity to make money on the game. Speculators were asking and receiving three to five dollars for their tickets. There were bets that Ottawa would win, that Renfrew would win, that Taylor would score, that Taylor would not. Renfrew was reported to have offered each of its players "a bonus if they play clean and avoid the penalty bench."[8] Odds were being offered that were two to one on Ottawa to win and one to two that they would double the score on the visitors.[9] Renfrew followers searched the town and the arena for such ventursome fools who were giving those odds, looking upon it as a sure windfall.

At least two hundred and fifty fans left the Valley town for the trip to the capital. Hundreds more were said to have trained in from other destinations, all anxious to see the confrontation. For those who couldn't attend, and had to stay in Renfrew, the Ottawa *Journal* made arrangements to provide a telegraph service which would provide bulletins direct from the arena. It was to be the first time that such a service was made available in Renfrew. Early Saturday morning, a lineman from Ottawa, together with a local technician, "ran the Canadian Pacific Railway Telegram Company wiring to Temperance Hall, connecting it with the telegraph outfit on the platform."[10] Later in the day, an Ottawa telegraph operator, Mr. McCanns, arrived on the evening train "and was right on the job at 8 o'clock to tell the Renfrew crowds how the spectators in Ottawa were roaring out a welcome to their favourites."[11] It was an elaborate system. McCanns was to take the news from the wire and relay it to an assistant, another *Journal* employee, who "announced the running story from the platform."[12] Yet another person was on the stage with a blackboard, writing out the "scores with the names of the men making them at the time."[13] A third newspaper employee oversaw the copying of the bulletins before they were sent to Easton's Cigar Store and to the nearby hotels. It was a dazzling operation, one which captured the imagination of the crowd with the wonder of it all, this instant communication of a scene sixty miles away!

Meanwhile in Ottawa the streets surrounding the Laurier Street arena were jammed. Every train that stopped at the nearby station poured out its human cargo: two hundred and fifty from Renfrew, one hundred from Brockville. . . all hurried up to the rink. A carnival atmosphere prevailed. Those with tickets clutched them, lest they lose them to the inevitable pickpockets; those without searched the crowded roads leading to the site in the frantic hope of purchasing standing room or whatever else a scalper might have available. And invariably, one could hear snippets of conversation rising above the din: "Taylor". . . "score". . . "backwards!". . . "traitor!"

Four hours before the game began, the line for standing room had formed. "By six, it extended to Albert Street and at seven, they were out as far as Queen and at 7:30 when the doors were thrown open, the snake-like chain extended to Sparks Street."[14] Once these doors were opened, there was a mad scramble for the best places. Some order was kept by the special detachment of police led by Inspector Gilhooley. Within minutes, the rush section was filled. Hundreds milled about, looking for a vantage-point. Behind the reserved-seat section, where standing room sold for seventy-five cents, people were lined up three and four deep. Later, they would be "jumping on each other's shoulders amidst the excitement for the purpose of getting a glimpse of the players as they shot up and down the ice."[15]

It was organized bedlam, the *Citizen* offering the slightly biased opinion that the "crowd was handled without a hitch."[16] High above, fans were perched on beams and rafters. Adventurous would-be spectators without tickets made their way up the outside of the building, "climbing along the roof, rubbering in through the open windows - one of which, on the west side, fell in and cut an Ottawa rooter's head so badly that several stitches were required. Dr. Nagle sewed up the wound and the enthusiastic fan, despite his injuries, stayed throughout."[17] The windows had to be kept open; there was a haze of smoke moving throughout the whole building, settling like fog over the ice. Once the windows were "opened, all signs of nicotine quickly disappeared."[18]

It's doubtful that anyone was ready for the display that followed. As the Renfrew players took to the ice, a chorus of boos accompanied them, growing louder as each one filed through the gate. When the last one, Taylor, left the dressing-room, the noise was deafening. Insults were shouted. Spectators throughout the building hurled expressions of "shocking vulgarity" from every corner. The noise, the stomping feet, the shouting, the "wild demonstration. . . fairly shook the building."[19]

Even once the game began, the display continued. "Lemons, oranges, and other fruit and a variety of other objects were hurled at the great player as he skated along the boards. At one point, a whiskey flask smashed at his feet."[20]

Play stopped. Players from both teams moved to clear the debris and broken glass from the ice, motioning Taylor to the relative safety of centre ice.

When play resumed, the abuse intensified: "Another shower of rotten fruit, copper coins, and shouts of 'Go home to Renfrew, Taylor. . . Back to the bushes. . . .'"[21] As the first half of play was coming to an end, with Taylor by the boards, another whiskey bottle, this one narrowly missing his head, was thrown from the stands.

If the Ottawa fanatics were trying to intimidate Taylor, he wasn't giving any such satisfaction to them. In fact, he was trying hard to shake off the two or three Ottawa players who were shadowing his every move, determined that their former team-mate would not score. And he did not - but he did manage to win the praise of many with his reaction to the onslaught. Indeed, as far as the players were concerned, it was a game, an intense one, but one in which personalities were secondary. Many times during the course of play, Taylor, who was close to the Ottawa bench, asked for and was offered towels to wipe himself dry or drinks to quench his thirst.[22]

Declared the *Citizen* of his spunky attitude:

*Seldom, if ever, has any athlete been forced to endure what Taylor was subjected to. To his great credit, it must be said that he bore himself remarkably well. Despite all the abuse and attempts to rattle him, he was at all times cool as a cucumber. He merely smiled at the hoots and hisses, showing remarkable nerve throughout.*[23]

At the end of regulation time, the score of the game was tied at five goals each. A ten-minute overtime, consisting of two five-minute halves, was agreed upon. Taylor, closely guarded all night, did not score; Renfrew goals were tallied by Lester Patrick with two, Frank Patrick with one, Hay Millar and Fred Whitcroft with one each.

The turning-point seemed to come in the second half. Frank Patrick had tied the score while Ottawa was short two men, their players tired from the extra work-load. The fans were hoarse from shouting encouragement to their favourites. Renfrew supporters, particularly those who had bet that Ottawa would not double the score, were on their feet looking for their team to apply the final blow. Players did not return to the ice from a penalty when a goal was scored. It was a tremendous opportunity for Renfrew to put the game away.

Suddenly Bruce Stuart, one of the penalized Ottawa players, returned to the ice. "Too soon!" said Renfrew's timer, George Martel. "Not at all!" countered Ottawa's representative, Rosenthal. The argument raged on, each timer refusing to concede to the other. By now, the players had skated to their respective benches. The crowd, thoroughly entertained by what would later be described as the finest game ever played in eastern Canada, sat still, quiet for the first time, in an effort to hear what was being said. In the end, the referee and Judge of Play decided to assume the task of timekeeper themselves. The Ottawa *Citizen* suggested that Stuart, whose return to the ice caused the dispute, may have played the trick deliberately, to rest his team.[24] Planned or unplanned, the tactic worked:

"Ottawa, well fagged, had a breathing space and got their second wind."[25]

Meanwhile, back in Renfrew, the Temperance Hall was as packed as the arena! The area around Easton's store was also crammed with throngs attempting to look over shoulders and through spaces to catch a view of the bulletins being posted in the store windows. High above the street, along the route from the hall to the store and from there to the hotels, where their runners brought them the scores as they were being posted, "Renfrew people stuck their heads out of the windows and shouted at them: 'how's the game now? Is Renfrew ahead?'"[26]

There was a holiday atmosphere throughout the whole town, an awareness that something of major importance was happening. It was out of sight but certainly not out of mind, not with this wondrous new technology they were all witness to. In an era when there was no television, when radio was still not used for such events and would not be for another ten years, the re-creation of events by a telegraph operator was wondrous! It shrunk distances, brought the outside world to Renfrew, emphasized the importance Renfrew was gaining - all because of M.J. O'Brien and his attempts to bring a Stanley Cup to the Ottawa Valley community.

The contrast between the crowd at the game and that at Renfrew was striking. Where in Ottawa's rink, there was almost a constant roar of noise, interspersed, indeed punctuated, with the disruptive throwing of debris or the hurling of epithets, at Renfrew there was a murmuring quiet, almost a hush, while they strained to hear the voice of McCanns as he reconstructed the game from the wire reports. "Though at times, there was great noise throughout the cheering . . . naturally interfered somewhat with the taking messages off the telegraph instrument."[27]

The experiment in Renfrew was a great success. The gathering was told of the huge crowd at the rink, the penalties, the tactics of each team and each scoring play. It was clear that Taylor and the two Patricks were on many people's minds.

"The audience was keenly interested in the announcements that two or three Ottawa men, all night, were especially watching Taylor."[28]

It was the second half of the game that really took hold of the Renfrew crowd. With their heroes ahead 3-2 the assemblage behaved "as orderly as could be expected when their favourites were doing so well,"[29] cheering and offering encouragement to a group of players sixty miles away who could not hear them. The cheering stopped abruptly with the announcement that Ottawa had tied the score. "'I guess Fred will win that one hundred dollars yet,' shouted someone,"[30] wishfully thinking or hoping that Taylor would come to the rescue, skating forward or backward, it really didn't matter, to score and put Renfrew ahead again.

It was an exciting, heart-stopping game; the constant action described by the telegrapher created all sorts of visions in his listeners' minds. Both teams were pulling out all stops:

*Toward the end of official time, when the score kept getting tied, four to four and then five to five, the excitement was at fever heat. The men were overheard saying they wished they had gone to the Capital but they sensed that their opinion of their chances of getting into the rink, with such a great demand for tickets, was so small. . .*[31]

With the end of regulation time and the score tied at five goals each, the news travelled quickly throughout Renfrew. There was "not one minute during the night that the score was not known all over Renfrew. . . Telephones in the hotels, stores and telegraph offices were kept busy."[32] Crowds thronged the CPR telegraph office which was the originating site of the information being sent to the Temperance Hall, Easton's and the hotels. The most popular person in town was Miss E. Cameron, who supplied the scores to those who simply wanted the bare essentials. She was said to have provided them in a way which was "reliable and there was never the slightest delay."[33]

Officials of the two teams conferred with the game officials to decide upon the overtime period. Would it be "sudden death" or two five-minute halves? The ten-minute option was agreed upon. It became obvious that the Senators were the fresher of the two teams. Perhaps they were more game conditioned than Renfrew. This was their thirteenth game and only the sixth for Renfrew.

The Ottawa tactics continued. Taylor continued to be effectively shadowed and not allowed to roam freely. Ottawa went on the offensive immediately. Frank Patrick was penalized. As in the Bobby Clarke/Valeri Kharlamov incident in the 1972 Team Canada/Soviet series when the soviet player's ankle ran into the Canadian player's stick, *The Renfrew Journal* reported, "Bruce Stuart, Captain and Rover of the Ottawa team, and perhaps the most valuable man they have, ran into Frank Patrick's stick."[34] Stuart fell heavily to the ice and was carried off in much pain. His collar-bone was broken and Stuart was lost to the Ottawa club for the season.

Ottawa scored three goals during the overtime session, each one with a man advantage. The final score was eight goals for Ottawa, five for Renfrew. Ottawa followers, most of them, were ecstatic.

And Renfrew? Not all of their supporters were downcast. There were those "in the north-east corner of the rink where the Renfrew crowd was located. A number of reckless Ottawans were separated from their cash as a result of betting that the Stanley Cup owners would double the score."[35] It was a foolish wager, advanced the home-town Renfrew paper, "when one considers the calibre of the men they were up against."[36]

That comment, despite its being made by a somewhat biased supporter, was typical of those expressed about the Creamery Kings. Taylor, regardless of the hostility of the crowd and the close play of his shadows, was said to have "put up a fine brand of hockey. Lester Patrick was another who was specially watched. Still, he managed to do fine work. Frank put up one of his star games. Lindsay, in goal, was a wonder worker and nice work nearly paid off."[37]

It took some time for the after-shock of the struggle to settle. Editorials appeared in the Ottawa papers expressing horror at the city's fans' reactions to Taylor and his team-mates. The *Free Press* labelled it a "despicable display"; Taylor was praised for his "admirable and courageous conduct." The *Citizen* was dismayed at the "terrible amount of abuse and punishment." It congratulated the former Ottawa star who "was physically bruised and battered from the beating he took on the ice as a marked man, but he was the first to offer congratulations to the victorious Ottawa players."[37]

In a lengthy interview with the *Citizen* after the game, the Cyclone gave "his own story of his experiences in the Renfrew - Ottawa struggle (which) would fill three or four newspapers." He declared that while he would not have missed the "strife of Saturday's battle, for love nor money," he preferred not to go through it again "until he forgets at least some of Saturday's scenes":

*I didn't mind the hooting, the hissing or the pet names they called me, but then that bottle landed with a crash a few yards away. I felt the joke had gone far enough. Made me think of a little old house up in Listowel and for a few minutes, I wanted to crawl through the roof. But my nerve didn't desert me for long and as soon as the play was started, I forgot the howling mob behind me and got down to work again.[39]*

The Renfrew players, too, were far from discouraged as a result of their defeat. They would "look for their revenge when the world's champions go to Renfrew on March 8."[40] Nine players would be carried by the Creamery Kings in anticipation of the strenuous games coming up. Frank Patrick was convinced that the difference in the game was the Ottawa goal-tender. Perhaps remembering the time when Ottawa first used him against the Wanderers, he offered the defence that: "Luck was against us or we would have beaten Ottawa. Talk about the man with the horseshoes! I'll take my hat off to

LeSueur any day."[41] Meanwhile, *The Renfrew Journal* was congratulating its namesake in Ottawa for the bulletin service which provided such welcome information on the important game to the Renfrew citizens. Basking in the glow of the thoroughly enjoyed, state-of-the-art service, it was "taken as proof that the name *Journal*, even in Ottawa, signifies enterprise in public spirit."[42]

Sunday was a typically quiet day in the Valley town. Families made their way to church services on foot, by wagon and in the odd car. Many of them detoured and lingered by Easton's Cigar Store, where the bulletins from the previous night's game were still posted.

NEWSY LALONDE OF RENFREW CLUB

# *Chapter Seven*

## *Newsy Lalonde*

Renfrew had little time to dwell on the loss to Ottawa. They had come close but they were outscored. Even so, there were still six games left, half the season, and the next one with the Montreal Canadiens was only three days away on the 15th. Who knew what would happen? Ottawa and the Wanderers still had to play each other and Renfrew had yet to play a return game with the Montreal team. O'Brien's dream of a Stanley Cup was not yet a nightmare; it was in trouble but certainly not dead. If it was going to expire, Renfrew officials would only let it die with a fight, some said a brawl, which at times seemed to be more of a flailing out, ready to grasp at whatever straw was available.

Renfrew seemed anxious to win the Stanley Cup even by proxy! George Martel floated the possibility that, in the event that Renfrew did not win the NHA championship i.e. the Stanley Cup, "the entire team would be handed over to Edmonton and played under the colours of that club in another series for the Stanley Cup."[1] That off-hand comment was a shocker. Newspaper reporters sought out the trustees for comment. Would this be possible? Would they allow this? Was Martel serious? Had he spoken to the trustees about this eventuality?

Trustee William Foran was quick to reply. No such deal would be allowed. Edmonton was certainly entitled to another challenge in the current year, if all the details could be worked out, but only with members of their team who had been with them throughout their current season and took part in their regular league games. "Eastern stars would be barred if an attempt was made to play them."[2] The story was described as "... one of the queerest that has been sprung ... for many a day, illustrating the keenness of the fight which is being waged for the possession of the Stanley Cup." The trustees comments were said to have "put the kibosh on the story altogether."[3]

Meanwhile in Montreal, where the Renfrews were visiting the Canadiens, the latter put up a spirited effort, hoping to catch the Renfrew team on the rebound. Though not noted for its rough play, the French club seemed to have picked up tactics from the Creamery Kings' previous opponents. Their spunky forward Newsy Lalonde was like a one-man wrecking crew, throwing his body recklessly at his opponents. On one occasion, "Lalonde and Taylor came together at great speed and first Lalonde went to the ice and then Taylor, as a result of the collision."[4] But Lalonde was more than a reckless, rough-house player. He had superb scoring skills. Invariably, in whatever league he was playing, he was the goal-scoring leader. He was there to score goals and was determined to remove any obstacles that would interfere with his objective. But he was more than just tough; he was shifty, fast, able to stop and start with quickness, and armed with an accurate shot. On this night, he shot four consecutive goals past Bert Lindsay. On one occasion, he skated down the ice with two point men between him and the net. Feinting a quick move in one direction, he went the other. "Taylor fell, giving Lalonde an easy opening." With Frank Patrick to get by, "he did it neatly, scoring from less than a yard out from the Renfrew cage."[5] Even though the Renfrew team had been short-handed at the time, there was no man-advantage on the play as far as Lalonde's goal was concerned. The goal brought the Montreal crowd to its feet. Even the Renfrew players shook their heads at the brilliant display by the fiery Frenchman. It showed the great skill that the Cornwall native displayed, game in, game out.

But the Montreal star was without much of a supporting cast. On that night, despite his four goals, Newsy's exploits were not enough. Renfrew prevailed, winning by an 8-6 score. Everywhere that hockey fans gathered, however, Newsy Lalonde was the topic of conversation.

So it was a great surprise, met with disbelief by all at first, that one day after the Renfrew game it was reported, "the star centre of the Canadiens, who distinguished himself by scoring four straight goals at the start of the match at the Jubilee Rink Tuesday night, has been released by the French Canadien club."[6] No reason was given for the move. Speculation by *The Gazette* was that Lalonde would probably go to Renfrew which "was in need of a good scorer. . . Lalonde can fill the bill. Certainly, he is not being released because of being considered a weak spot on the Canadiens' team."[7] There is no indication that the newspaper had any inside information about any possible deal but it was certain that there had to be a reason other than the traditional one given when players were released. The Ottawa Senators agreed too. They were quick to offer the scoring ace three hundred dollars per week for the remainder of the season.[8] It would mean at least four pay-cheques. To nobody's surprise, in Montreal anyway, Lalonde declined the offer and became the newest member of the Millionaires.

Ottawa, rebuffed, signed Walter Smaill, who had left Cobalt because of a contract dispute with that financially struggling club. But whereas Lalonde was welcomed with open arms by his new Renfrew team-mates, the same was not true of Smaill and his new Ottawa club. Captain Fred Lake and Hamby Shore were rumoured to have threatened to leave the Senators if they carried through with their plans to replace Ken Mallen with the former Cobalt star when they met the Wanderers in Montreal. Mallen, a youngster who had impressed many with his speed and stick-handling ability on the right-wing, had only played one game but scored two goals. The Ottawa executive decided to go ahead anyway, preferring the established veteran Smaill. It was an inopportune time for dissension to break out in Ottawa. Playing the Wanderers in their next game after Renfrew, February 19, and with Smaill in the line-up, the Senators lost their first game of the season, a 7-5 decision to the Wanderers.

There was no such dissension on the Renfrew team. They were thrilled to have the colourful Lalonde with them. Not only was he a goal scorer, teams would think twice about running at Taylor and the Patricks with Newsy there. In fact, it was Frank Patrick who was partly responsible for the club having signed the irrepressible Frenchman. After the last game with Ottawa, Renfrew's dressing-room took on the quiet atmosphere of countless dressing-rooms after a loss in a big game. It seemed to be time for reflection, each player mentally replaying the contest, looking in his own soul to see if anything more could have been given. As Frank Patrick sat, alternately thinking and peeling off his uniform wet with the perspiration of effort, a Renfrew executive approached. Was the Stanley Cup out of the question, he asked? What could Renfrew do to improve their chances of winning the Cup? Patrick's answer was quick: "If we could get a player like Newsy Lalonde, we'd still have a shot at it!"

Patrick and Lalonde had formed a mutual-admiration society many years ago, born out of the joy of effort each one expended in games they saw each other play. Both were approximately the same age, Frank was one year older. Rarely had there been a better example than Lalonde of someone who was able to succeed by combining raw talent with clawing-and-scratching combativeness. When Lalonde was a member of the Toronto Maple Leafs in the 1908 Ontario Professional Hockey League, he was the scoring leader. The Leafs, as champions, challenged the Montreal Wanderers, holders of the Stanley Cup. The trustees agreed to a sudden-death contest.

Frank Patrick was then a defenceman with the Montreal Victorias. At the same time, he was a referee with the ECHA, the youngest, some said the best. He had torn a shoulder ligament and missed the last two games with the sixth-place team, but he was still able to officiate. The young referee was noted for his hockey knowledge and his ability to take charge of a situation; he was assigned to the Wanderer/Leaf Stanley Cup game. In its own right, it was a difficult task, made even more so by the fact that many of the Montreal players knew him as a young amateur; there was a fear that they would attempt to take advantage of him.

The game was close. The Wanderers were leading by one goal, 4-3, when a Toronto player was injured. Patrick called a time out. Maple Leaf attendants came out onto the ice to minister to the team member who was in pain on the ice. The ever confident Wanderers, playing at home, looked around the arena. Some skated over to their bench, others gathered in a knot on the ice while still others looked around the rink to see who, in the crowd, they could visit. Three of them, Art Ross, Walter Smaill and Riley Hern, the goalie, skated over to the boards to have a chat with their girl-friends sitting in the front row.

With the Toronto player's recovery, and the return of the trainers to the bench, most of the Wanderers had returned to the ice. Patrick blew his whistle to call the players to the face-off circle in the Toronto end. The three Montreal players, still visiting, ignored the call. Patrick blew his whistle again! Still the three players, apparently aware of their inflated self importance, continued to linger with their ladies. Patrick wasn't having any of it. He decided to drop the puck, thinking that by the time it was moved into the Wanderer end, the three would have hustled back into position.

Meanwhile it was Lalonde, the Toronto centre man, who was in position, poised to take the face-off, anxious for Patrick to drop the puck. When he did, Lalonde gained the draw and quickly fired it down the ice towards the empty net. The crowd was screaming. The three players, snapped out of their reverie by the shouting crescendo, all made a dash for the net! Too late! Lalonde, his face now in the broadest of grins, had scored the tying goal. There were debates and arguments that threatened to go on all night but Patrick stuck to his decision, thankful later, however, that the Wanderers had gone on to win six-four, sparing Patrick any further confrontations. However he remained quite impressed with Newsy and his ability to be completely involved in the game. He was happy that such a versatile player would be a team-mate.

About thirty Renfrew citizens joined the hockey team aboard the two private railroad cars leaving for the two-game swing in the silver country. Everywhere, there was renewed enthusiasm. Another genuine star had joined the team. More importantly however, there was the certainty that this one would allow the others to perform even better, making for a superior team!

The Cobalt game was "by no means a parlour exhibition."[9] In fact, it threatened to deteriorate into a wide-open no-holds-barred brawl as the visitors moved into a seven-two, half-time lead. Renfrew eventually won the game by a twelve-goals-to-seven score. Lalonde scored four goals, the Patricks six - five for Lester, one for Frank; Bobby Rowe scored one as did the Cyclone, who seemed content to play a defensive role, making the odd scintillating dash, but preferring to let the others carry the offensive load. The Cobalt players were in a foul mood throughout the game. There were rumours abounding that the team had not met its payroll; the players were doubly frustrated with the appearance of the Millionaires and their fancy guaranteed contracts. Cobalt had lost its best player, Smaill; Renfrew went out and bought another superstar, Lalonde, and as far as the Silver Kings were concerned, that was done after the association's deadline for players moving from one team to another. The old CHA regulation date had been January 30 and that was certainly in the past. There was some disagreement as to whether the new NHA date was February 15, as Cobalt believed, or that none had been approved, as Renfrew thought. In any event, Cobalt launched a protest to be heard at a league meeting called for February 28. Notwithstanding all of that, it was cold!

Meanwhile, in Renfrew, the town was again able to follow the progress of their team in Cobalt with the Ottawa *Journal's* bulletin service. A special CPR wire had been installed at the E.W. Easton store. From there, the information was relayed to the rink, scene of a high-school game between Renfrew and Ottawa collegiates. There, "the story was told by a *Journal* representative with a megaphone,"[10] to the one thousand in attendance. Even with the high enthusiasm,"it seemed to be a foregone conclusion with the Renfrew people that their team would win at Cobalt with the final score not a great surprise."[11] At Easton's, the Saturday night crowd gathered around the bulletin board, which brought the scores not only from Cobalt, but also from Montreal and the Renfrew rink. It was said to have "attracted a larger crowd than the one on Saturday night one week ago."[12] Indeed, the newspaper proudly reported: "'Hockey seasons after this cannot be complete without a *Journal* bulletin service', declared a member of the Executive of the Renfrew Club after the games had been concluded."[13]

The Creamery Kings' next game was against Haileybury on February 22. By then, Ottawa's loss at the hands of the Wanderers was well-known. Newsy Lalonde was indeed working his magic. It represented a second chance for Renfrew. Ottawa could have clinched the Cup, had they defeated Montreal. Now, those two teams were tied; Renfrew still had a game apiece with each of them. The Stanley Cup was back in their sights.

But first things first. Haileybury was next on the agenda and any team which had Art Ross on it was always going to be a threat. Not only that, they had one of the most physical teams in the NHA, to go along with their great scorer. And playing in the north country had its own perils: the cold weather for one, and the rough-and-ready patrons who came to the games ready to back their boys in every way.

That Tuesday night of February 22 might have been the coldest night on record for a hockey game. The temperature was -25°F! There was such a cold arctic wind blowing out of the north that it seemed much colder than that. It was an era before wind-chill factors were taken into account but there was no need to inform the players or the spectators that it was much colder than even the thermometer could record. Spectators brought whatever they could to warm themselves, from the outside in, or, even more popular, from the inside out! There was no prohibition in Haileybury, although some argued that there should have been. Players dressed in long johns, extra sweaters, hats, gloves, anything which could keep them warm. Thankfully, the walls in the arena, shaped like a huge airport hangar, and appearing to be of temporary construction, nonetheless served as a wind-break against the blasts of wintry air.

How cold was it? Art Ross appeared on the ice wearing a tuque which he had pulled down over his face, much in the style of a Balaclava, two slits cut out where his eyes were. On his hands were a pair of fur mitts. He looked much bigger than most of the players remembered him, undoubtedly from the extra layers of clothes he wore. He looked very menacing, much like an evil apparition.

During the course of the game, Ross collided with Lester Patrick clubbing the Renfrew player on the jaw with his stick. The Renfrew captain, never one to back down from any intimidation, retaliated in kind. Ross appeared momentarily stunned. Recovering from his surprise and regaining his balance, Ross separated himself from Patrick and moved away a short distance. He dropped his stick and gloves, circling the Renfrew player much like a boxer stalking his opponent. Within a very short time, the Haileybury player, always well-known for his common sense as well as his scoring prowess, stopped and suddenly bent down to scoop up his gloves, putting them back on his freezing hands. Lester could only laugh in amazement at what was happening. That occasion stayed in hockey lore for many years as the only fight "called on account of cold."[14]

Several players were treated for frost-bite during the course of and after the game. Still, it continued, watched by a large crowd who had come to see their favourites playing against this team they had heard so much about. They were dressed in whatever could be found to keep themselves warm, fortified by coffee mixed liberally with whisky. Each Haileybury goal was an occasion for wild and unrestrained enthusiasm; each enemy tally was followed by a murmuring discontent - and a shower of whatever was available to throw on the ice.

One particular fan was most obnoxious. Not only did he shout obscenities at the players as they skated close to the boards in the area where he was perched, he would also shove a stick through the wire screen in an attempt to poke them. Renfrew players had become aware of him and had warned each other of the habit, wondering aloud as to why such fans were allowed into the game. He seemed to be especially primed to goad Taylor and when the Cyclone was sandwiched between two Haileybury players, causing him to fall heavily to the ice, the fan jumped up next to the screen. He pounded on the mesh with his hands, all the time shouting a stream of obscenities at the dazed and windless Cyclone. He moved along the boards, ignoring the spectators who were between him and where he was heading. When he reached the area directly above where Taylor lay, he hovered over the writhing form, separated only by the screen which his face pushed against, the steady torrent of abuse continuing.

Frank Patrick, normally a mild-mannered individual, bent over his team-mate, disgusted at the individual. Suddenly, he wheeled, the butt-end of his stick smashing against the screen in the exact location of the insensitive screamer's face. A splatter of blood spurted from his nose and sprayed the screen, boards and ice. The suddenly quieted disturber slowly slumped out of view.

In the game itself, Renfrew took an early 3-2 lead at half-time. The team seemed to undergo a definite improvement when Fred Whitcroft replaced the injured Hay Millar after the intermission. They played with more enthusiasm; only time would determine how big the margin was to be. But there had been anxious moments too.

During the first half, "Lindsay was struck in the eye with the puck and his optic closed."[15] There was a twenty-minute delay. Again, there were some fans who took the opportunity to bait the southerners. Lindsay was in no shape to continue. Renfrew executives and players huddled to consider strategies. One of them spotted Cobalt's goal-tender, Chief Jones, in the crowd. Quickly, an emissary was sent to the fan to ask him if he would consider playing goal for the remainder of the game. Not only that, they would give him two hundred dollars and assured him that they would straighten out any league problems that might arise. Jones, pleased at the thought of playing in nets for the Millionaires and earning an unexpected windfall of two hundred dollars, agreed. He went to the Renfrew dressing-room to change.

Meanwhile Tommy Hare, the Cobalt manager, was also in the crowd watching all that was developing. He was livid. He had already lost Walter Smaill; he had protested the use of Newsy Lalonde by Renfrew and still they persisted in playing him; Jones was still under contract to Cobalt and there was no way that he would be allowed to play for the visitors. Besides, there was enough natural antagonism and rivalry between the two mining centres of Cobalt and Haileybury. Who needed any more? He had to live in the north!

Again, the Renfrew officers brought out their wallets. Some said that they thought they could get whatever they wanted with their money. Hare was offered one hundred dollars to allow Jones to play. The Cobalt manager was adamant! There was no way! He ordered his goalie out of the dressing-room.

"The Chief by this time was climbing into a Renfrew uniform. He took it off and returned to his place in the rink as a spectator."[16] It might have been the first and only time that a Cobalt player ever received a standing ovation from a Haileybury crowd! Lindsay was forced to return to his position "between the nets but had to retire again in the second half for another twenty minutes."[17]

Bert Lindsay's gutsy play, his "grand game,"[18] was a big factor in the 11-5 Renfrew victory where rough play continued to mar the proceedings. When it was obvious that Whitcroft's substitution had given the Creamery Kings a lift, Haileybury sought to intimidate him. "Whitcroft was cross-checked by Gaul shortly after he replaced Millar and lost several teeth. After that, he hardly played up to form."[19] By that time, however, the spark had taken hold. Lester Patrick and Newsy Lalonde each scored three goals to lead the attack.

After the end of the game, the Renfrew team returned to the dressing-room, wanting to leave the crowd behind as quickly as possible. It had quieted somewhat, having gained a grudging respect for the Millionaires who seemed to be able to play the game in whatever style the opposition dictated. Even after Frank Patrick butt-ended the foul-mouthed fan, Art Ross skated over towards him, hunched over with his stick across his knees, and surreptitiously offered his congratulations and thanks for having quieted the trouble-maker.

Indeed, as Patrick showered, he was informed that the Haileybury sheriff was asking for him outside of the dressing-room. Fearing the worst, the thought occurring to him that his father Joe might hear of his anticipated trip to the hoosegow, the youngster dressed slowly. Visions of spending a long, cold night in the Haileybury jail house flashed into his head.

His fears were in vain. The sheriff simply wanted to shake the hand of the player who silenced the spectator who had been a source of discomfort to most Haileybury supporters all season long! Again, the story was added to the ever growing, long list of lore that was developing among players wherever they would meet.

Meanwhile, as the hockey team was out of Renfrew for its fourth consecutive road game, preparations were being made to expand the Argyle Street rink before the next three home games, but especially for the Montreal Wanderers and the Ottawa Senators. Major renovations were under way to raise the seating capacity to "three thousand from the present two thousand."[20] A new gallery was to be erected and "one side was to be torn down to make room for the extra seats. . . .The management of the hockey club also own a large share of the stock of the rink and intend to spend several hundred dollars for alterations."[21]

As if to put the cap on the events leading up to the big game of the season, an announcement was made that Renfrew's Patron of Everything had donated a beautiful silver cup to the National Hockey Association. The O'Brien Cup was to be awarded to the league champions. It was described as "magnificent . . . worth six hundred dollars.:. a masterpiece of the silversmith's art. . . made entirely from the O'Brien's silver mine in Cobalt."[22] Three trustees were named: Harry Tihey, Emmett Quinn, and T. Yates Foster of Montreal. Perhaps it was a recognition that the Stanley Cup would not always be available for the NHA champion, that the league should have its own trophy. The ever optimistic Renfrew *Journal* reported: "This fine trophy and the Stanley Cup are the honours worth striving for and the Renfrew hockey team is doing nicely at that alright!"[23]

Nicely indeed! And the pivotal games of the 1910 season were both going to be in Renfrew. First were the Wanderers then Ottawa. And there was still that make-up game with the Shamrocks plus the final game of the season with Cobalt.

It was probably fitting that the pivotal game of the 1910 season, the one which would determine the Stanley Cup, would be in Renfrew. After all, these two teams, Renfrew and the Wanderers, were the original members of the NHA! They had been party to all the condescending comments and put-downs from the CHA clubs. They had not only seen the breakup and demise of the rival league, they were also part of the tremendous growth and acceptance of the newer NHA - and they had both witnessed the bended-knee approach of the Senators and the Shamrocks! They had proven to everybody that they knew what they were doing, that they had been right all along.

True, Renfrew and its aggregation of millionaires had gained most of the headlines, but the Wanderers were one of the finest teams ever, anywhere, anytime! Ernie Russell, just a mite of a man at one hundred and forty pounds, was as accomplished a football player, with the Montreal Amateur Athletic Association (MAAA), as he was at hockey with the Wanderers. A fast skater and accomplished stick-handler, he was equally at home as a centre or rover. In 1907, he outscored the great Russell Bowie, netting forty-two goals in just nine games! This prolific scorer had had two eight-goal games, three six-goal games, and had scored five goals on four different occasions, most recently against the Shamrocks on February 9. By 1910 he had already played on three Wanderer Stanley Cup teams and was looking forward to his fourth!

Russell's line-mates, Harry Hyland and Jimmy Gardner, were also making reputations for themselves. Hyland was only in his second year in professional hockey. He broke in with the Shamrocks in 1909, scoring eighteen goals in eleven games. With the Wanderers in 1910, he was showing that he could still put the puck in the net - no sophomore jinx for him! He would better his scoring output of last year. In a later game with the Canadiens, he counted five goals. Jimmy Gardner was more of a checker and a role-player as the third member of the forward line. One of the older players at thirty, he had already played as a Stanley Cup champion in 1902. During the 1909 season, he had a personal high of eleven goals and was right on course for a repeat season during 1910. Pud Glass, at rover, was another small but aggressive player who captained the team. He was noted for his ability to set up his team-mates but could also put the puck in the net. In 1909, he had scored seventeen goals. He also had a ten-consecutive-game scoring streak going into the Renfrew game.

On the point (defence) was Ernie Johnson. He had begun his career as a speedy left-winger on a line with the other Ernie Russell, and Glass. That line led the Wanderers to three consecutive Stanley Cups in 1906, '07 and '08. It was only during his seventh season, 1910, that he had been moved to defence and paired with Jack Marshall. Johnson's trade mark was his stick which seemed longer than everybody else's because of his long sweeping poke-check. It seemed even longer when combined with his elongated arms. The six footer towered over his smaller mates, giving further credence to the lore. Newspapers of the day portrayed him with rubberized, stretching arms because of the effectiveness of his poke-check. There were already legends growing about the man who would be better known to some as Moose. He played hard, off and on the ice, and had the grudging respect of all, friend and foe alike.

Jack Marshall, his defence mate, was a rink-wise veteran who was content to protect his end of the ice rather than attempt to score goals. He too had been with three previous Cup winners: 1901 with Winnipeg, 1902 with the Montreal AAA and in 1907 with the Wanderers.

The eighth man was forward Cecil Blachford. He always seemed to be in the background but was a recognized leader. He had been captain of the Wanderer teams when they were Stanley Cup champions in 1906, '07 and '08. Although never a high scorer, he was invariably able to average a goal a game throughout his long career. After the 1908 season, he retired. His team-mates presented him with the Arena Cup, emblematic of the ECHA championship. With the formation of the NHA, the other players prevailed upon him to end his retirement, turn professional and join them on their journey to yet another Cup season.

The goalie of the team was Riley Hern. The native of Stratford, Ontario, joined them in 1907 and backed them to Stanley Cups in that year and 1908. In an era when high-scoring matches were common, he had a respectable goals-against average of 3.4. Some of his detractors felt that anybody who could stand (goal-tenders were not allowed to leave their feet), could tend the Wanderers nets - their combination of good scorers and superb defence would win them most games. But Hern, like all of his club members, with the exception of Pud Glass and Cecil Blachford, was later elected to the Hockey Hall of Fame!

On Friday afternoon, the day of the match, the 1:40 train from Montreal arrived at the Renfrew station. A special car was attached to the end of the long line of those pulled by the now quieted and hissing steam-engine. Curious onlookers had gathered. They had heard much about the Wanderer team but, for many, this was their first opportunity to see them in the flesh. "Never before has there been such excitement in Renfrew as there is today,"[24] reported the *Journal*. The whole town was aware of the big game and the excitement could be felt everywhere. If the smallest youngster was asked what was happening, he "would laugh and say: 'Oh, did you not know that Renfrew plays the Wanderers tonight?'"[25]

Indeed! Just one hour after the arena ticket-office had opened on Wednesday, all reserved seats were sold. Even with the expansion having been completed, the new balconies almost doubling capacity, it was a foregone conclusion that not everybody who wanted to would be able to see the contest. All seats were sold by 6:00! There simply would not be enough space to satisfy those who would have to settle for standing room.

And the crowds were still coming! Each train brought in its human cargo from Pembroke, Arnprior, Ottawa, Montreal, Brockville and Eganville. When the special from Pembroke and the regular Ottawa train arrived at the same time, "the street was filled with people from the station to the rink."[26]

Along the roads connecting Renfrew with its smaller neighbours, people were walking or were carried by carriage from Burnstown, Springtown, Spruce Hedge, Black Donald, Goshen, Haley Station, Admaston, Douglas, Cobden, Mount St. Patrick, Dacre and a host of farming communities in between. All were eager to see the game in which "more interest was taken than at any other time in the season."[27] The "country people . . . showing great interest, (were) coming in loads from two to fifty!"[28]

Hockey was *the* topic of conversation. The two victories by Renfrew on their northern swing through the silver country and the new addition of Lalonde had rekindled excitement. The players had each professed themselves to be "in the pink of condition."[29] Only Millar was said to be "suffering from a severe attack of the grippe,"[30] but he was expected to play. The scuttle-butt had the Wanderers replacing Hyland with Blachford, but the Renfrew players weren't about to believe that. "They think Hyland the much better man on the form he has been displaying in the past few matches."[31]

The Creamery Kings were established as three-two betting favourites. After all, they were the home team; their jaunt through the north had been a success; there was a certain aura that had been built up about them because of the intense publicity that they always seemed to generate no matter where they were. "There's a lot of Renfrew money in sight but so far, no large bets have been put up," lamented the *Journal* reporter on the day of the game. The Wanderers, befitting a veteran championship team, maintained their poise and did nothing that could be used as ammunition against them. Regardless of the odds, they said, they "expected a hard contest but hope to win out."[32] With the Renfrew team said to be "just as confident, it will be a battle royal between two of the greatest hockey teams in the world."[33]

By 8:00 pm, the Referee and the Judge of Play had been appointed. They were members of the Montreal Victorias, one of the greatest amateur teams of then-recent history. When news circulated that Duncan Campbell and Russell Bowie had been appointed, it spread like wildfire; the huge crowd roared its approval. It was an opportunity to see one of the greatest hockey players ever. Bowie was legendary. Over a ten-year period, he played eighty scheduled games and scored the amazing total of two hundred and thirty-four goals! Almost three for every game he played! He could have made a fortune had he decided to turn pro, but he chose to remain an amateur, retiring after the 1908 season. The two officials had earned a reputation as the best in the business. They had so much control, there was almost a guarantee of a clean game. It was just another indication of the importance of the game to all.

By 8:30, the advertised starting time, the rink was full. There was some impatience for the game to start. A feeling of tension was everywhere throughout the packed arena. Even before the game began, there was "real rooting from the Renfrew rooting brigade. . . . The boys are cheering as if the teams were playing."[34]

Both teams appeared with their usual line-ups. The Wanderers took to the ice first, led by Pud Glass and accompanied by a rousing cheer. Next came Renfrew, led by Taylor. They were "cheered to the echo,"[35] but there was also a moment of disbelief. Was someone playing a joke? As the Renfrews took to the ice, they were wearing the uniforms of the Rivers, the amateur team! As the teams skated their warm-ups, the explanation began making its way through the buzzing arena. Both teams had red and white-coloured uniforms. The Wanderers had brought only one set, whether by design or accident, forcing the Creamery Kings to wear the strange outfits. There really wasn't much that Renfrew could do. The rink was full; the ice was in the pink of condition. Everything seemed set for the most important game of the season. The Renfrew players were accustomed to seeing the Rivers' uniforms during their practices. The amateur team practised with them often, the session usually ending with a scrimmage between the two sides. Perhaps they had conditioned themselves to think that the Rivers' uniforms were to be avoided. In any event, a reporter observed: "Some of the Renfrews are dressed in coat sweaters, the rest are dressed for action. . . Renfrew appears strange in the new uniforms."[36]

When Russell Bowie called the two captains together for the coin toss at the beginning of the game, a great cheer went up form the crowd. Lester Patrick won it and chose to defend the north goal. It was 8:35. It was the last thing that Renfrew won that evening. Bowie dropped the puck between Lalonde and Russell and the Montreal Wanderers skated off to a resounding 5-0 victory!

# *Chapter Eight*

*The Millionaires.*

There was now only a slim, outside chance that the Renfrew Creamery Kings could win the Stanley Cup. The game with the Wanderers had been a shattering experience, a great blow coming off the club's two great wins in the north. To all appearances the team, under the coaching of Alf Smith, had finally jelled. The addition of Newsy Lalonde was universally taken to be the final ingredient in the mix. Excuses, or rather, reasons for the loss and the lack of any goals, were sought. Could it have been the amount of time spent on the train? The frigid, strength-draining temperatures of the north? The strange uniforms? There was no intent to down play the Rivers but the professionals looked more like the amateurs on that Friday evening. Oh, there were a hundred excuses that one could offer but the real reason, that eventually everyone came around to, was the Montreal Wanderers! They were a magnificent team, with the heavy emphasis on *team*. They had played together for years; they could score goals and they could stop them! They were the type of team that could play the game at whatever pace and in whatever style needed; they were more than good, they were superb! Their little men skated all over the ice; they might have been the best forecheckers in the business. Twice, they took the puck from Taylor in his own end and twice they put the puck past Lindsay as a result. And if you got past their forwards and were able to move into the Wanderers' end, Moose Johnson and his point partner Marshall were right there, ready to play it however you wanted. That pair wouldn't back down from anyone!

And so in Renfrew it wasn't so much that the townspeople were down on their boys, it was more that they had nothing but admiration for what was being called the finest team in the world. There was only hope that the Renfrews would recover their scoring touch before their next home game with Ottawa on March 8. Even *The Globe* had observed, "Renfrew played as if they were all off their form."[1] The newspaper ventured the opinion that the results of the Wanderers game would "likely sound the death-knell of professional hockey in Renfrew, for with their team hopelessly out of the running, it is difficult to see where the club is going to get its patronage. . . . An explosion in the league may now be looked for."[2]

*The Globe* was simply expressing the concerns that all leagues, but particularly professional ones, have. Will the fans keep coming out when the chances for a play-off spot or the possibility of winning the championship have been eliminated? And there were concerns! On the one hand, with the top contenders during the last couple of weeks, the crowds had never been so good. The Renfrew/Ottawa game had attracted a huge assembly, over seven thousand spectators, the largest ever. When Ottawa travelled to Montreal to play the Wanderers on February 19, it was obvious that the small Jubilee rink, with its capacity of two thousand, seven hundred, could not accommodate the large number of those who wanted to attend. Arrangements were made to hold the game at the arena with its capacity of six thousand. The smug looks, about the switch, of "We told you so," on the Ottawa faces, were obvious. Every seat, every space, in the arena was filled for the pivotal game. And of course, the Renfrew rink had added more than twelve hundred seats in anticipation of its upcoming Montreal, Ottawa and Cobalt games.

On the other hand, however, there was some concern as to whether Cobalt and Haileybury would finish out the season. They had losing records and not only that, there had been a great deal of money lost in gambling. When Cobalt went to Ottawa for its February 26 game, the players threatened to default for the rest of the season: they hadn't been paid, Walter Smaill had gone, prospects for the future looked dim. A reorganization of the club saved the day, at least for the remainder of the year - a reorganization that, some said, bore the fine hand of the O'Briens. Messrs M.T. Culbert and H.P. Glidden of the O'Brien Mines, one of the Noah Timmins family, and Mayor Lang agreed to underwrite all expenses, past and future, for the remainder of the year. The arrangement was well received throughout the league, but especially in Cobalt where the last game of the season featured a visit of arch-rival Haileybury on March 15.

All of these matters were discussed at an NHA meeting on February 28. They could easily have been explained away as the time of the year. Ice rinks were dependent upon the weather; there was a hint of spring in the air, the weather was turning mild. And the Stanley Cup was all but settled, at least as far as the majority of clubs was concerned. It would have been easy to throw in the towel and drop out of the competition. But they didn't. Perhaps it was the performance bond that each club posted at the beginning of the year. More likely, however, it was because of the competitive games left to play with their rivals. In any event, all teams decided to carry on.

Some unfinished business was also resolved at the meeting. Ottawa's signing of Smaill and Renfrew's of Lalonde were approved by the league. The continuing saga of Bad Joe Hall reappeared and was also resolved, albeit in a different way. Hall, who had been fined by the league for attacking Judge of Play Rod Kennedy, refused to pay the one-hundred-dollar fine! There was also a matter of $27.50 to cover the costs of repairing the official's clothes, ripped during the scuffle with the Shamrock player. Hall refused to pay that too! The Shamrocks were forced to pay all on his behalf. Furthermore, the Association ordered that the tie game between Renfrew and the Shamrocks was to be replayed on neutral ice in Ottawa on March 2. It was subsequently cancelled because the warm weather had caused the ice to melt. In any event, fan interest in Ottawa seemed low since both teams were out of contention. This combination of circumstances forced the NHA to drop the game.

Meanwhile, the focus of Renfrew shifted to Ottawa. There was still a home game to be played with the Senators on March 8, a chance to gain a measure of revenge. Before that, there was a chance to watch the Stanley Cup champions against the Wanderers. The March 5 game, at the Laurier Street arena, represented another chance to scout the opposition and, at the same time, observe the wondrous Wanderers once again.

The game was all that it was built up to be. The Wanderers, once again, displayed their superb talents. Led by their two Ernies, Russell and Johnson, they won by a 3-1 margin, clinching the Stanley Cup. It was their fourth in five years! Trustees Ross and Foran made arrangements to prepare the trophy prior to its being shipped to the victors:

*. . . left an order this morning with A. Rosenthal and Sons Ltd. for the first improvements that have ever been made to the Stanley Cup. The present base of the famous trophy is carved and marked up to such an extent that further names could not possibly be put on it. Consequently, the trustees have ordered a new base for the Cup and, also, a new silver ring which will provide space for engraving for many years.*[3]

The Stanley Cup might have been out of reach but there was still the March 8 game to be played with Ottawa. Any contest with that club was sure to create interest. It was like David and Goliath all over again: There was little Renfrew, with its population of three thousand, versus Ottawa and its eighty thousand! At the same time, the pressure was off. The Cup was gone. There was only some lost pride to salvage.

Two events stood out prior to the big game. One was the birthday of Charlotte Whitton. Lottie was the Renfrew team's unofficial mascot, a favourite of the players. Her fourteenth birthday was being celebrated on March 8 and, in honour of that, the players had agreed that, as a gift, they would welcome her on the bench for the Ottawa game - Queen for the day! The other event concerned the irrepressible Newsy Lalonde.[4]

The newest member of the Renfrew Creamery Kings had a reputation as a most competitive person, ready and willing to contest anything and everything, anywhere and at anytime. In addition, there were countless references to his closeness, some said tightness, with his money. He was reputed to be so tight that when he took a dollar bill from his pocket, the king squinted! On a Monday, the day prior to the Ottawa game, after the morning work-out, Lalonde and Larry Gilmour decided to walk over to the O'Brien household. M.J. was out of town, in Mexico, looking after his mining interests there. Ambrose was home. The three, roughly the same age, enjoyed passing the time of day with each other. Gilmour, the young home-brew, was carried mostly for his insurance value, in case one of the players was unable to play. Lalonde, cocky and self-assured, had the supreme confidence about him that he could do anything, and better than anyone else. Ambrose was good-naturedly enjoying his role as owner but also friend to this magnificent group of young men.

Fresh snow had fallen and was still on the ground. The three enjoyed a leisurely light lunch and conversation in a room overlooking the open spaces, glistening with its winter whiteness. There seemed a desire to talk about anything but hockey. The topic eventually turned to snow-shoeing. Out of the blue, Lalonde challenged Gilmour to a race on snow-shoes - for five dollars! Perhaps Newsy was trying to spook the young rookie. After all, five dollars was still a lot of money to the young local. To Lalonde, however, it was a drop in a very big bucket. He was said to have been signed for two thousand dollars for the remainder of Renfrew's season. Anyone knowing of Lalonde's reputation for his reluctance to part with money would have concluded that the cocky little Frenchman was confident of his ability to beat Gilmour in a snow-shoe race.

Gilmour was nonplussed. He agreed almost immediately. Ambrose let out a hearty laugh, as if he knew something! He would be the referee!

The ground rules were established. The race would be for approximately three miles. A farmhouse, south of Renfrew on the way to Dacre, was chosen as the finish line. Ambrose would give the signal and follow in a cutter, judge the fairness of the event, make the presentation, and squeeze the two aboard for the ride home.

At the start, the two moved very deliberately, yet quickly, ahead. Ambrose flapped his reins gently, moving the horse parallel to the two contenders. After a short distance, Newsy noticed that Gilmour was not a novice to the sport. He was moving effortlessly, with little strain and much co-ordination. After a third of the distance had been covered, it was obvious that Lalonde was overmatched. He would have to part with his five dollars!

Meanwhile Gilmour, the superb athlete that he was, continued merrily on his way. He was inwardly grinning at Lalonde having played right into his hands. This would be the most enjoyable five dollars that he had ever won. When he was a couple of hundred yards ahead he stopped, turned, laughed and gave an exaggerated bow, hat in his hand, towards his tiring adversary. O'Brien, aware of Gilmour's prowess on snow-shoes and the circumstances, relishing all with gales of laughter, was positioned between the two, catching the looks on both their faces.

Lalonde called upon every ounce of muscle and will-power in his reserve and picked up his pace. Form was thrown to the wind. Arms pumped and legs churned carrying the snow-shoes up and down, forward and back wildly in an effort to beat

Gilmour - and win the bet. Suddenly, there was a tangle of arms, legs and shoes. There was a frantic, muffled yell. The ace scorer had tumbled and lay in the snow, motionless. He was grasping his ankle; low moans emanated from his throat. O'Brien reined in the horses. He stopped the cutter, jumped down and raced through the deep snow to the stricken Lalonde. Gilmour, now aware of what had happened, came flopping back hurriedly.

Newsy was groaning. He strained to control his writhing. He pointed to his ankle, his right one. The owner and team-mate uttered an inaudible curse. The ankle looked as if it could be broken. Lalonde could be gone for the remainder of the season. The injured snow-shoer was lifted gingerly onto the cutter and wrapped in a fur to keep warm. With great effort, his face contorting with every move, the game competitor reached into his pocket and pulled out a five-dollar bill. He extended it to Gilmour.

O'Brien intercepted Lalonde's outstretched hand. He refused to allow the injured party to pay, saying that if he had not been injured and was able to continue, it appeared as if he might have caught Gilmour. The other competitor nodded his assent. O'Brien reached into his own pocket and took five dollars out, passing it on to the "winner." He told Gilmour that there wouldn't be room on the cutter for all of them. He must get Lalonde back to the house to see a doctor quickly. Gilmour would have to follow as best he could.

The two sped off, Gilmour trudging behind. Lalonde turned once, pained look on his face disguising a faint grin. He waved at Gilmour who was wearily trudging back to the house. When the cutter made it back, a doctor was summoned to examine the ankle. It was a strain, not a break. The best treatment for it would be ice and rest. They would just have to re-examine and test it tomorrow to see if Newsy could play.

To nobody's surprise, really, he could. In fact, he made a remarkable recovery. Gilmour couldn't believe it. Ambrose O'Brien was amazed. And pleased too! Sure, the Stanley Cup was out of the question but Tuesday night, March 8 represented another chance to rub Ottawa's nose in it. M.J. was still away but he and his dad thought much alike. He proposed some added incentives for the team, "$100. to be divided among the players for each Renfrew goal, plus $50. to the scorer!"[5]

Whether the incentives had any effect on the game can't be said. But, who cared? Lottie Whitton could not have had a better birthday present. The Renfrew fans, more than three thousand of them, were on their feet throughout, thoroughly enjoying the outpouring of sheer power. It was a rout! Seventeen goals for Renfrew and only 2 for Ottawa! Newsy Lalonde had recovered remarkably from his "broken" ankle, damaged while trying to win, or rather, not lose, five dollars. He had gained an additional three hundred dollars plus his share of the seventeen hundred in bonuses, scoring six goals! Lester Patrick had counted four, Taylor three, Millar and Frank Patrick, two each.

Finally, the team had clicked. *The Renfrew Journal* reported it as "one of the fastest exhibitions of hockey ever seen on local ice, at least on one side."[6] It was a time for crowing:

*It was the worst score that has happened in Professional hockey for many a day. Just 17-2, that's all. From the very start, Ottawa was completely outclassed with Renfrew players simply skating all around them. Despite the hardest work and the best game Ottawa could put up. Ottawa never got a worse trimming.*[7]

If Perc LeSueur had been the "man with the golden horseshoes," as he was described by Frank Patrick after their first meeting, the Renfrew players had learned to shoot through them for the second. "From the very start, every Renfrew player played a wonderful game of fine hockey, each man doing his part to perfection."[8] Indeed, according to the Renfrew newspaper, Ottawa had played as well as it could. Renfrew simply outclassed it. "Ottawa and Renfrew had good reason, alright, to be proud of Tuesday night's great game."[9]

Of course, there were other reasons bandied about to explain the result. There was talk that, with the game not meaning anything as far as the Stanley Cup was concerned or for that matter the standings, Ottawa had done its share of celebrating before the game and was feeling the ill effects of its indulgences. It was also suggested that perhaps the Renfrew players were better performers later in the evening. It was after 9:30 when the game had started. The spectators began to get edgy because of the delay.

The late start was necessary because one of the officials due to work the game, Bob Meldrum, had missed his connecting train in Ottawa, from Montreal. The Senators wanted to name the second official. Renfrew objected "on principle to the double-header idea from Ottawa while not at all criticizing any of the officials personally."[10] Eventually, Renfrew won the right to designate its choice, "Mr. Jordan, of Quebec, now residing in Renfrew."[11] There was no indication that the Renfrew player and O'Brien employee, Herb Jordan, showed any partisanship in his officiating.

But the talk of the town was not the officiating, not the fiery Frenchman, Newsy Lalonde, not the Patricks, nor the little girl sitting on the players' bench - no, not even the scoring of seventeen goals while holding the Senators to two. The main topic of conversation was the Cyclone. He was a little late but he finally made good his boast of scoring a goal while skating backwards! It was late in the game, the contest had been long decided. Taylor picked up the puck in his own end and raced towards the boards cutting sharply up ice. He isolated the point men with a feint inside and moved around them. In just a few strides he was alone in on LeSueur. He pivoted around, his back to the goalie and while continuing backwards, lifted the puck past the startled Ottawa net-minder! Even the Ottawa fans applauded that one!

Renfrew had one more game to play, with Cobalt, on Friday. That game was recalled much later at a reunion dinner for the

Millionaires. It was hosted in Ottawa by the Prime Minister, John Diefenbaker:

*Before the game, I tell Lester that it would be terrible if a great player like me don't win the scoring championship, and Lester, who was the Captain, agreed. He asked me how many goals I need to win the title. Of course, he knows how many I need, but, I think it over anyway. I said, I need eight goals to win, and Lester think it over, talks to the other guys and says, Okay, Newsy, we see that you get eight goals. That shows me you can't trust anybody. I got nine goals but with a little help, I could have scored at least a dozen!*[12]

Newsy did indeed score nine goals and won the league scoring championship with, according to *The Globe*, thirty-four goals,[13] and to Charles Coleman,[14] thirty-eight. All agreed, however, that Newsy Lalonde won the title, that the game was a rout. Renfrew won it by a 15-4 score, in spite of the fact that it chose to play some of its younger players like Eddie Hogan and Larry Gilmour. The latter, who doubled as the team manager when he wasn't playing, was the recipient of a nasty cut on his face, courtesy of Harry Smith's stick. An interesting coincidence was that Cobalt's goalie, Chief Jones, was hit in the face by a puck shot by Hogan, much like Lindsay was in the Haileybury match. He was virtually unconscious for fifteen minutes but was forced to continue when no substitute was available.

Renfrew's NHA season was complete, but not so for Cobalt. It had to return home for its final league game on Tuesday, March 15. As it turned out, it was the final NHA game played by the two teams, Cobalt and Haileybury. The rivalry was typical of the two silver communities in everything, whether or not the Stanley Cup was on the line. In the first meeting between the two teams, Cobalt's Harry Smith was the centre of attention, as much for the use of his stick as a weapon as his goal-scoring ability. The game was in Haileybury. As its players kept going down, victims of Smith's stick, Police Chief Paddy Collins was called. Smith was arrested and taken to jail.

In spite of that, Cobalt won the game by one goal, 7-6. Haileybury's stick victims recovered and Smith was released.

The rematch was the most discussed event of the time. It was estimated that some two thousand paid their way into the Cobalt arena. Every conceivable spot was taken up. The betting was furious. Noah Timmins, the Haileybury sponsor, was said to have wagered fifty thousand dollars on the outcome. Cobalt supporters scrambled to take portions of the huge bet. Some were too nervous to watch the contest, preferring to walk off their tension in the cold night air. Each burst of ecstatic cheering brought them back in to see what had happened. At half-time, Cobalt supporters were jubilant; their team was ahead 5-0!

Noah Timmins was not amused. He burst into the Haileybury dressing-room at half-time. He was angry; he demanded a better effort!

The team responded. Led by Art Ross, Haileybury shut down Harry Smith and his Cobalt mates. At the same time, they scored five themselves to tie the game. Overtime was necessary. Sudden death was agreed upon: the first goal would win the game. Once again Timmins went into the dressing-room. This time, his words were encouraging; he offered one thousand dollars to the Haileybury man who scored the winning goal!

*The tension in the arena was unbearable. Both teams had game-winning scoring chances but goalies Chief Jones of Cobalt and Billy Nicholson of Haileybury came up with brilliant saves. Finally Art Ross passed to Horace Gaul who shot the puck past Jones. Haileybury had won!*

*From the galleries, crowded with Cobalt supporters, there came cries of despair. Suddenly from the weight of humanity, the railing collapsed; many fans tumbled fifteen feet to the ice and some were so seriously injured that they had to be taken to the hospital on sleighs.*

*The hysteria continued. Winning fans showered pennies, dimes, quarters, even dollars on the ice. The air was filled with greenbacks and the players were trying to catch their floating fortune on the fly.*

*But Billy Nicholson somehow had obtained a tub and any money iced in his vicinity was quickly snared and "tubbed". When he could find no more loot, and the sweat was pouring from his brow, he calmly turned the tub and its contents upside down and sat on it so that no one could dislodge him or the money. How much money he collected,"Nick" never admitted, but there were guesses that he wouldn't have to work for a long time.*[15]

In the last NHA game of 1910, on March 15, Cobalt was unable to gain its revenge. It lost to Haileybury, 14-9.

# Chapter Nine

## "World Champions"

*Moved by Reeve Harry Moss, seconded by Mr. Cox:*

*WHEREAS certain well-known citizens of the town of Renfrew have interested themselves in Professional hockey and expended a large sum of money in procuring and maintaining a professional team of the very best talent to represent Renfrew in the National Hockey Association during the season of 1909-1910 and*

*WHEREAS one result of the action of these citizens has been to give enjoyment and pleasure to a large numbers of our citizens of smaller mean, both men, women and children, who have delighted in seeing the chiefest of Canada's winter sports played by the exponents of the game in Canada and,*

*WHEREAS a further result of the town of Renfrew has been advertised in a manner never before attempted and the leading papers throughout the country have reported the doings of the hockey team from day to day and thereby made the town of Renfrew known with a reputation from the Atlantic to the Pacific, and*

*WHEREAS the players that represent Renfrew during the past season have proved themselves to be worthy of the citizens of the town during their stay with us,*

*Frank Cosentino*

*We, the Town Council of Renfrew, tender to the said hockey players, the executive of the Renfrew Hockey Club and financiers, a banquet to be held after the return of the hockey team from New York city, and, that the Mayor and Messrs. Cox and Ritza, be a special committee to make the necessary arrangements.*

*CARRIED* [1]

The proclamation was introduced and passed at the March 14 council meeting. Immediately, it set into motion a chain of preparatory events, which had to be accelerated because of the shortage of time. The team had been invited to New York city. There it would play the winner of an Ottawa/Wanderers two-game series before returning to Renfrew and dispersing.

Again, the community was stirred up. No, the Stanley Cup wouldn't be at stake, but the Wanderers were the acknowledged world champions. They had embarrassed Renfrew by a 5-0 score, and right in its own home rink. News reports from New York were eagerly sought-after and discussed throughout the town. The Wanderers had extended their mastery over Ottawa, winning two games by identical 4-3 scores in Tuesday and Wednesday-night games "of the most brilliant kind."[2] To make the Renfrew/Wanderers contest even more interesting, a purse of fifteen hundred dollars was to go to the winner of the Saturday, March 19 game.[3]

Before leaving for New York that midday of Friday, March 18, the players were paid off for their season's play - in cash! "The salaries in all amounted to above sixteen thousand dollars, Lester Patrick at twenty-seven hundred, being the highest-paid man. Frank Patrick drew two thousand and Fred Taylor, two thousand."[4] About forty officials, supporters and players made the trip, including Lindsay, the Patricks, Taylor, Rowe, Millar, Whitcroft, Lalonde, Hogan, Jordan and Fraser.[5] *The Globe* commented, somewhat enviously: "the Millionaires will travel in their usual sumptuous style, a private car, big party of followers, etc.."[6]

Indeed, it was from this time on, after the players had been paid their huge cash settlements prior to their trip to New York, that they became more commonly referred to as the Millionaires, rather than their official club name of Creamery Kings.

Certainly, it appeared that New York was eagerly anticipating the arrival of "the Millionaires team, comprising the highest-paid players in the Dominion."[7] They seemed to be particularly enthusiastic about the fact that it seemed necessary for Ottawa and the Wanderers to merge their best in order to challenge "the powerful Renfrew professionals."[8] It was to be a fitting climax to the New York hockey season. St. Nicholas Arena, with its artificial ice, had long been home to hockey, but the players it attracted for its league games paled in comparison with the outstanding teams brought in at the end of the season. "The Renfrew players are noted for their exceptional skill, having been picked from the best professional teams in the Dominion."[9] And as far as the New York papers were concerned, the foremost of the best was "Jeffries" Taylor, "the man who is paid ten dollars for every minute that he is on the ice. Considering that he is paid $5,000. for playing just a dozen games, he is unquestionably, the highest-paid player in team sport. His salary shames what is paid our star baseball players for a full 154-game season."[10]

This was Taylor's third visit to New York in the past three years. People anticipated his coming; he had a huge following, not only because of his wondrous hockey ability, but also because of his resemblance to former heavyweight boxing champion Jack Jeffries! Hence the Jeffries Taylor appellation.

For the other players, New York was another world: the tall buildings, the number of cars on the road, the subway, Times Square, the theatre district, the great number of languages heard on the streets, the five-cent beer, the felt bowler hats, Broadway. . . . Although the game was being played on artificial ice at St. Nicholas Arena, with its capacity of six thousand, five hundred, there was also great interest in

Madison Square Garden. It did not have an ice surface yet, but it seated ten thousand! It was of particular interest to the Patricks. Just two years later, they would open up the first artificial-ice rinks in Canada, in Vancouver and Victoria.

A full house was at St. Nick's. There were the rabid and the curious. Senior hockey had been played on the artificial-ice surface for years. For the last two, Ottawa and Montreal had sent their best teams to compete for a purse of one thousand and fifteen hundred dollars. Everybody was happy with the arrangement. The players were treated royally and got to display their talents before an appreciative throng; the promoters were guaranteed a full house, something that sowed the seeds for a future NHL team; and the fans were treated to a display never before thought possible.

As for the game itself, Renfrew jumped into a 7-1 lead at the half. It was a dazzling display. The fans were absolutely enthralled, never having witnessed such talent and against a team which, only a few days ago, they were calling the best in the world! They had adopted the Millionaires as their own, mesmerized by the great skill of the Renfrew players from Canada (some Renfrew players were confusing the New Yorkers, telling them that Canada was in Renfrew!). The fans were still amazed by the look-alikes, Fred "little Jeff" Taylor and Bobby "Teddy Roosevelt" Rowe. The latter player had damaged his eye early in the game and was forced to wear protective glasses, "the crowd proclaiming him at once as Teddy Roosevelt, refusing to believe anything else."[11]

It was one of those games where every Renfrew player demonstrated his immense talents. The whole team was just now beginning to jell, playing as all had thought they would during the season. "Lalonde, hailed as the champion scorer of the world, lived up to his good reputation. . . Frank Patrick, Millar and Rowe, all put up great hockey. . . Lindsay, in goal, was good indeed, as the score showed. . . Lester Patrick was another special star and his work was especially efficient. . ."[12]

But it was for Cyclone Taylor that the accolades were most effusive: "He took New York by storm alright, as a hockey player. His brilliant, graceful dashes down the rink, caught the public fancy to a 'T'."[13]

The second half was even more exciting than the first as the Wanderers attempted to redeem themselves, determined to live up to their previous weeks' performances as the Stanley Cup champions. As a result, "the play, in the second half, fairly scintillated with brilliant performances. . . it was neck and neck all the way in this period, both sides fighting like demons. . . "[14]Never before had anything like it been seen in New York. The spectators were on their feet almost throughout. Each play seemed to create yet another level of performance previously unimagined:

*the play was strenuous and fierce. . . the penalties, handed out right and left. . . a constant procession to the timer's bench. The feature was the play of the two cover-points, Taylor and Johnson, generally considered to be the two greatest men to have ever donned skates. Their work was simply marvellous. It would be hard to choose between them as they play much different, at the same time, such effective games, that a comparison is hard to make.*

*Taylor is undoubtedly the most spectacular of the two and his end-to-end rushes fairly swept the crowd into enthusiasm. His cyclonic rushes, his sudden stops, his brilliant checking and great rushes demoralize the opposing seven.*

*On the other hand, Ernie Johnson was in every play all over the ice. First at one goal, then at the other, down on his back, flat on the ice and up again in a second, always in possession of the puck and his long reach and poke at the puck broke up play after play in the most bewildering fashion. He was almost the whole team in himself!*[15]

Renfrew won the game outscoring the Wanderers by 9-4. "The New York press hailed Renfrew as the Champions of America, which means the Champions of the world. . . as one paper put it, 'they beat the second best team in the world.'"[16]

As far as the team and its supporters, who journeyed with them to New York, were concerned, it was said to be, "the finest time and the best trip of the season.. They had an elegant good time. . . . The boys can't say too much about the generous way in which the management supported and looked after their comfort and pleasure."[17]

Meanwhile, the plans of the "Municipal Council of Renfrew to tend to the Renfrew Hockey Team, their financiers and executive, the Rivers hockey team and management, a complimentary banquet, as a mark of appreciation for the fine sport given the town this year,"[18] hit a snag. The team was due to return from New York on Tuesday March 22; many of the players had made arrangements to leave for their homes the next day. Word reached the town on the Tuesday afternoon that the banquet would have to be that evening if the town wanted to have the players in attendance! A moment of panic set in. Surely the town would be remiss if it could not honour this group of men for "the fine advertising that has resulted for Renfrew through this magnificent all-star aggregation of hockey players who upheld Renfrew's name in the National League. . . practically acknowledged in New York, where they won a big purse, to be the best hockey team on the continent."[19] For a while, it appeared that the hockey banquet, which at one time was said to have been in danger of being cancelled "because Lester Patrick and Cyclone Taylor can't agree as to which shall propose the toast to the girls of Renfrew,"[20] might have to be set aside.

There was only one thing that could be done. The dinner would have to be held that Tuesday evening! A regular municipal banquet could not be held - there simply was not time. Councilmen Cox and Ritza had to move fast. They and their committee decided that "by no means should the World Champions, who have brought such honour to Renfrew, go unhonoured."[21] They swung into action.

Phone calls were placed to Ottawa to arrange for a "caterer to assist the local experts at this end. Ballantyne's famous orchestra was secured. . . assisted by Mr. Chas. Johnstone on the piano."[22]

When the 6:40 arrived from Ottawa, "the team, the caterer, much of the material for the banquet and many other necessary features of the evening,"[23] were aboard.

There was a mad rush to obtain and decorate a hall in order to have the banquet. Mackay's, at the corner of Raglan and Elizabeth Streets was available. Decorating proceeded at a furious pace, and the hall was soon bedecked with "streamers and emblems on the walls. . .(telling) of the successes of the Renfrew hockey team."[24]

All of the Renfrew players were there, "with the exception of Mr. Ed Hogan, who was unfortunately called home from New York, owing to his business place being destroyed by fire."[25] There was no mention as to whether alcohol was served as part of the celebrations, although there were certainly many toasts; Renfrew was a dry town at the time. In any event,"after a social time, the guests sat down at the well laden tables and after repast had been enjoyed, a toast list was taken up,"[26] under the direction of Mayor Arthur Gravelle, toast-master for the event.

Not only was the evening an opportunity to celebrate the town's two hockey teams, but especially the Millionaires, it also gave its top citizens the opportunity to wax eloquent on what the hockey team had meant to the community that they all loved. In his opening remarks, Mayor Gravelle made a "brief but happy speech."[27] It was brief because it was almost midnight before the speeches and toasts had begun. He expressed his "appreciation" for the "fine sport. . . given by the two best teams in the world." He was indeed "grateful for the good advertisement given this town". He would always be thankful for "these good sportsmen, financial backers and supporters, who had done so much to give the people the pleasure of this high-class sport." He was much aware that "the town was heralded from one end of the continent to the other."[28]

With the end of the singing of "God Save The King," a toast to the monarch was made by Mr. David Barr and Dr. Bernard Connolly, members of two of the longest-settled families in Renfrew. Mr. Barr observed, "credit had been done to Renfrew's name through the length and breadth of the land," by the team. He gave his thanks for the prosperous and peaceful reign of the present king and "happily expressed the general gratitude of the loyal subject and hoped that the present sovereign would be spared to reign for many years."[29]

Dr. Connolly offered his congratulations to the town for "the splendid class of sport. He felt that those who had not taken an active part in hockey matters of the team, owed a debt of gratitude to those who had so generously supported this fine advertisement and amusement with their money, time and ability."[30]

The toasts continued. Former MP A.A. Wright "made one of his characteristic speeches, full of wit and liveliness."[31] The last such dinner in honour of one of the town's sporting champions, that he took part in, was in 1905. He was a Liberal Member of Parliament from Renfrew at the time. On that occasion, the Renfrew Lacrosse team had won the championship of the Ottawa Valley, and the prestigious Citizen Shield. Long after the dinner was over, after midnight, celebrants gave the Sporting Editor of the Ottawa Citizen, Dr. Mellon, an impromptu ride around town in a borrowed delivery wagon.[32]

Councillor W.A. Moore hoped to see the Stanley Cup next year; John Mackay, pleased to represent the "mercantile establishments," spoke of the two teams "in which the greatest pride was justifiable."[33] Mr. James Clark and Mr. M. Devine also spoke, the latter commenting that the schedule had been "rather hard on Renfrew."[34] The evening took on an appreciation of the town of Renfrew itself. The "professions" were toasted: Dr. French "made a bright and pleasing reply,"[35] followed by J. Charles Johnston, "who was much interested in Renfrew's success, although circumstances had prevented him from ever seeing a scientific game of hockey."[36] Legislators Thomas W. McGarry, MPP, and Thomas Low, MP, "aptly responded" to the "toast of the Parliaments."[37]

McGarry, a lawyer and avid curler, "gave one of his inimitable and eloquent addresses, full of bright sallies and apt illusions and well turned phrases." Saying that he was proud of the teams and the financiers, he knew "from his own experience during the session in Toronto, that the team had spread the good name of Renfrew to all the corners of the Province and beyond." Moreover, it was especially pleasing, he said, because the team members"were such perfect gentlemen and being so, did honours always to the town."[38]

The tributes continued. Thomas Low, MP, spoke similarly. He called upon personal anecdotes much to the delight of those in attendance. He also "expressed the general regret at the absence of M.J. O'Brien, one of Renfrew's best citizens and a man who was ready to support sport or anything else that would add to the pleasure and the profit of the people of Renfrew."

Councillor Harry Cox praised the team "both as men and players." He extolled Renfrew as a place where the "well to do had a fine and democratic spirit." Where else was it common to see a "millionaire driving a load of wood down . . . streets?"[39]

More toasts! To the Press! To Andrew Carnegie and New York! More speakers! Messrs Jackie, Plaunt, McKinnon and MacDonald all repeated the happy theme: the good time in New York, the fortune that Renfrew had to have such good men and executives on their team, the great benefits to Renfrew, the advertising from coast to coast and throughout the continent.

When the players were asked to say a few words, their every word was sought-after and listened to. When the guests were toasted, all looked to young Ambrose O'Brien to respond. The son of M.J. declined and asked to be excused because of a heavy cold. The enthused audience, many of them having spent some time speaking with the honoured citizen during the social time, understood. Still, they continued to lavish praise upon him at every opportunity. Jim Barnet rose to reply. He expressed his thanks and appreciation to the town and its citizens, as well as his regret at not having won the Stanley Cup. However, "as it was, in winning the New York game, the team brought back an honour that was never before brought to any town of this size in Canada."[40]

One by one, the players rose. Herb Jordan spoke of the great appreciation the players had "for the invariably kind and generous treatment received from all the people in general." Jordan, from Quebec, had already decided to make his home in the Valley town :"'Renfrew's good enough for me,' said Mr. Jordan."[41] Some of the players were shy and said very little, Edouard "Newsy" Lalonde, Larry Gilmour, Hay Millar, and Bert Lindsay, in particular. Fred Whitcroft, a reporter when he lived in Edmonton, praised the members of the Renfrew papers, the *Mercury* and the *Journal*, for their fine coverage.

It was a long evening. Yet there was genuine affection expressed - both ways. There was a heartfelt sorrow that the season was over, that next year was far away, that the moment might never again be captured. The citizens of the town had enjoyed the young men who were part of their community during the all too short hockey season. Frank Patrick was very moved when he "spoke feelingly of the fine treatment accorded the hockey players all through the season."[42] Fred "Cyclone" Taylor shared a reply to the "toast to the ladies." Both he and Frank agreed, "there were no finer anywhere. The players would be willing to return next year and play for nothing if the Renfrew girls were still here."[43]

It was Lester Patrick who commanded the rapt attention of all. His eloquence was widely appreciated by the seventy in attendance. When he broke into his practised rendition of one of Drummond's poems, done in a French Canadian patois, the gathering was hushed. Their attention was riveted on the fluently bilingual captain of the Millionaires:

*W'en I was young boy on de farm, dat's twenty year ago*
*I have wan frien' he's leev near me, call Jean Bateese Trudeau.*
*An offen w'en we are alone, we lak for spik about*
*De tam w'en we was come beeg man wit' moustache on our*
*mout'.*

*Bateese is get it on hees head, he's too moche educate*
*For mak' de habitant farmerre - he better go on State -*
*An' so wan summer evening we're drivin' home de cow*
*He's tole me all de whole beez-nesse - jus' lak you hear me now.*

*'W'at's use mak' foolish on de farm? dere's no good chances lef'*
*An' all de tam you be poor man - you know dat's true you se'f*
*We never get no fun at all - don't never go on spree*
*Onless we pass on 'noder place, and mak' it some monee.*

* * *

*I see Bateese de oder day, he's work hees fader's place*
*I t'ink mese'f he's satisfy - I see dat on hees face*
*He say "I got no use for State, mon cher Napoleon*
*Kebeck she's good enough for me - Hooraw pour Canadaw."*[44]

There was a loud ovation. His "really excellent elocution fully deserved the reception."[45] In his remarks, he again thanked all and apologized for the team not capturing the Stanley Cup. No other town, except perhaps Edmonton, would ever hold such an evening for a losing team, he thought. The whole season had been an education for all. He was sure that all knew now where Renfrew was, although, referring to the gullibility of the New Yorkers and the fun the players had had with them, he wasn't sure whether they thought that Renfrew or Canada was the country's name. Patrick said that he preferred the former, earning laughter all around.[46] Then, acceding to the wishes of the crowd, he finished with yet another rendition about Bateese.

It was a long evening, but a happy one. The *Mercury* reported, with some feeling:

*They are not ordinary birds of passage of the type familiarly associated in the minds of the public with much professional sport. Some of them are men of business standing, whose occupation leaves them free in the winter, as well as men of education and ability and while much idle time is always a danger, the group have conducted themselves here, so far as the* Mercury can learn, as to win the respect of the citizens as well as their hearty admiration as expert exponents of a fine winter sport.[47]

The *Journal* was similarly impressed by the evening which closed with "God Save the King" and "Auld Lang Syne." "The banquet went off without a single hitch and the whole evening was a complete credit to all connected with the management of the affair."[48]

The whole community had been enriched by the Renfrew Millionaires!

# *EPILOGUE*

At the end of the 1910 season, M.J. O'Brien removed himself from Renfrew's hockey fortunes. He had other interests and his hockey losses had been substantial. His memory in the sport was perpetuated by the O'Brien Cup awarded to the NHA and later NHL champion until it was replaced by the Prince of Wales Trophy in 1927. It now resides in the Hockey Hall of Fame in Toronto. O'Brien's contributions to Canadian life were so many and so varied that he was appointed to the Senate in 1918 by Prime Minister Sir Robert Borden. In 1926, he was honoured with a Papal decoration, Knight Commander of the Order of Saint Gregory the Great, for his support of charitable and religious institutions. Perhaps one of the most telling things about this millionaire was that his word was his bond, high praise for anyone whether in the world of sport or outside it! He died in November, 1940. The town of Renfrew was virtually closed for his funeral; flags flew at half-mast, schools were closed so that the children could attend his funeral.[1]

Ambrose, his son, continued his involvement with the Millionaires for the 1911 season. Even though the team ceased operations after that season, Ambrose's contribution to hockey was recognized with his election to Canada's Hockey Hall of Fame (see appendix C).

There were changes during the 1911 season. The NHA had decided on a salary cap of five thousand dollars per team for the season! It was a far cry from the heady days of 1910 when money was being spent liberally, much of it due of course to Uncle Imjay. It was a huge drop for everyone but particularly for the Renfrew players. Indeed, throughout the NHA, it provoked threats of withdrawal of services and, if necessary, the formation of a new league operated by the players themselves. The latter fell through; the various clubs had tied up all of the arena time in their respective cities. There was nowhere for the players' league to play. Reluctantly, they returned to their clubs, signed the new contract developed by the NHA (see appendix B),and resigned themselves to playing for lower salaries.

There were other changes. The Patricks stayed out west and formed their own Pacific Coast Hockey Association in 1911. The teams in Vancouver, Victoria and New Westminster took advantage of player discontent in the east and attracted many of the top performers. As well, the Patricks, benefitting from their travels and from the help of their father's lumber interests, built the first artificial-ice arenas in Canada, in Vancouver and Victoria.

Meanwhile, in the 1911 NHA season, Newsy Lalonde returned to the Montreal Canadiens; Whitcroft and Millar went back to Edmonton, retiring after the 1910 season, as did Eddie Hogan. Jack Fraser departed for the Maritimes. Renfrew's hockey team for the 1911 season was comprised of Bert Lindsay, Bobby Rowe, Herb Jordan, Larry Gilmour and Fred Taylor from the 1910 team. Taylor had taken to wearing a cap, covering his prematurely bald head. His play at times seemed only a shadow of his former ability; some were referring to him as "the old man,"[2] especially after the team lost a game to Ottawa by a 19-5 score.

Considering the salary cap, Renfrew attracted some good young players to the team. The other members of the 1911 club were Odie Cleghorn, Sprague Cleghorn (a future Hall of Famer), Jack Gillerain, Harold McNamara, Skene Ronan, Don Smith and Steve Vair.

There were also some changes in franchises for the 1911 season. Cobalt and the Shamrocks dropped out; Haileybury's franchise was transferred to Québec City. The name Canadiens was challenged by George Kennedy, owner of the Club Athletique-Canadien. He sought admission to the NHA and wanted to use the Canadien name, threatening a lawsuit. The NHA granted him a franchise that he continued to call Les Canadiens, and reverted the original Canadien franchise to Ambrose O'Brien. For 1911 then, the NHA consisted of the Ottawa Senators, the Montreal Wanderers, the Montreal Canadiens, the Quebec Bulldogs and the Renfrew Creamery Kings. A sixteen-game schedule was drawn up. Ottawa regained the Stanley Cup; Renfrew finished tied for second place with an eight-wins, eight-losses record.

After the 1911 season, Renfrew's second in the NHA, more money was lost. The team was withdrawn from the 1912 schedule. Ambrose O'Brien sold his two franchises, the Renfrew team and the original Canadiens, to Toronto interests. However, it would be 1913 before the two Toronto teams, the Torontos and the Arenas, would enter the league, delayed because of Mutual Arena construction problems.

In 1911 the game began to take on its more-modern characteristics. Three periods of twenty minutes each, with ten-minute intermissions, replaced the two thirty-minute halves. By 1912, the seventh man was eliminated and unlimited substitution was allowed. It was a cost-cutting feature as much as anything. In the west, seven-man hockey was still being played. The PCHA attracted many established performers including former Renfrew players Lester Patrick, Frank Patrick, a rejuvenated Cyclone Taylor, Bobby Rowe, Newsy Lalonde and Bert Lindsay, father of future NHL Hall of Famer Ted. The calibre of play was so high that by 1917 the Seattle Metropolitans, an American team with Canadian players, won the Stanley Cup. The Stanley Cup was now a trophy of international status.

Later that year, in preparation for the 1918 season, the NHA became the NHL. All the owners had withdrawn from the NHA, not wanting to associate with Eddie Livingstone, the owner of the Toronto team, and formed the new league without him. His franchise was taken over by the Arena management. Four teams began the season in the new National Hockey League that now played its first games in December: the Ottawa Senators, the Montreal Wanderers, the Montreal Canadiens and the Toronto Arenas. The Wanderers were unable to finish the season; their arena had burned down. The Toronto Arenas won the NHL championship and the Stanley Cup when they defeated the Vancouver Millionaires in a play-off between the PCHA and the NHL. Perhaps it was a proxy victory for Renfrew and O'Brien.

And Fred "Cyclone" Taylor and his girl Thirza Cook? By March 1914 he had saved his ten thousand dollars. Taylor's team, the Vancouver Millionaires, arrived in Ottawa to play an exhibition series with the Senators, prior to leaving for a New York tournament with Quebec and the Wanderers. On the afternoon of March 14, 1914, he married Thirza in a quiet ceremony in her home. Frank Patrick was his best man. Taylor was to continue his legendary play in the west. In 1949 he was awarded the Order of the British Empire for "outstanding service to his country and community as an immigration officer in two wars."[3]

When the town of Renfrew celebrated its centennial in 1958, surviving members of the Millionaires were invited back to be honoured at a reunion of the team that had made the Ottawa Valley community famous. Prior to that, Prime Minister John Diefenbaker had "hosted a dinner in the Parliament buildings honouring the remaining members of the Renfrew Millionaires."[4]

Taylor, the Patricks, Newsy Lalonde, Fred Whitcroft, and Sprague Cleghorn were all later selected to the Hockey Hall of Fame (see appendix C). Ambrose O'Brien was similarly honoured in the Builder category.

In Renfrew today, there are few visible remembrances of the days when Butterville or O'Brienville, as Renfrew was likely to be called, was widely known because of its hockey team. True, there is still an O'Brien Road, an O'Brien Park and the O'Brien Bar and Grill in the Renfrew Quality Inn. The hotel, opened in September, 1988, was constructed on the site of one of O'Brien's World War I munition plants. The O'Brien Opera House was closed and the building was converted to an apartment house. The O'Brien theatre is still next door. But the dreams of a Stanley Cup are only a hazy vision of long, long ago!

# *Appendix A*

| Renfrew 1910 | | |
| --- | --- | --- |
| **Name** | **G.P.** | **Goals** |
| Lalonde, E. | 11 | 38 |
| Patrick, L. | 11 | 22 |
| Rowe, B. | 9 | 12 |
| Taylor, F. | 12 | 10 |
| Jordan, H. | 6 | 9 |
| Millar, H. | 9 | 9 |
| Patrick, F. | 11 | 8 |
| Whitcroft, F. | 5 | 3 |
| Fraser, J. | 4 | 1 |
| Gilmour, L. | 2 | 0 |
| Hogan, E. | 1 | 0 |

Goalie
Lindsay, Bert   12   54
GPA 4.5

Coach
Smith, Alf

| Renfrew 1911 | | |
| --- | --- | --- |
| **Name** | **G.P.** | **Goals** |
| Smith, D. | 16 | 28 |
| Cleghorn, O. | 16 | 20 |
| Vair, S. | 12 | 13 |
| Taylor, F. | 16 | 12 |
| Rowe, B. | 16 | 10 |
| Cleghorn, S. | 12 | 5 |
| Ronan, S. | 3 | 3 |
| Gillerain, J. | 2 | 0 |
| Gilmour, L. | 3 | 0 |
| Jordan, H. | 1 | 0 |
| McNamara, H. | 6 | 0 |

  16   101
GPA 6.3

# *Appendix B*

## *Contract Adopted by*

## THE NATIONAL HOCKEY ASSOCIATION OF CANADA

This Agreement, made this . . . . day of . . . . 1910 between. . . . party of the first part and. . . . party of the second part, Witnesseth:

First:- Said party of the second part agrees to devote his entire time and services as a hockey player to said party of the first part during the period of this contract.

Second:- Said party of the Second part agrees to conform to all the rules and regulations now adopted or which may be hereafter adopted by the party of the first part appertaining to his services aforesaid.

Third:- Said party of the second part agrees not to render any services as a hockey player during the time of this contract to any other person, corporation or association other than the party of the first part, without the written consent of the party of the first part to do so.

Fourth:- It is further understood and agreed between both parties to this contract that all the provisions and conditions of the Reservation clause of the National Hockey Association of Canada are hereby made a part of this contract.

In consideration of the foregoing promises, the party of the first part agrees:

First:- To pay to the party of the second part the sum of $.... per game, month of season to be paid in equal weekly, semi-monthly instalments during the championship season of the league of which the first party is a member.

Second:- Said party of the first part agrees to pay the travelling expenses, board and lodging of the said party of the second part whenever said party of the second part may be travelling in the services of the said party of the first part and when not so travelling the party of the second part will pay all his own expenses.

Third:- Said party of the first part agrees to furnish said party of the second part with one, only, complete outfit for his use while employed with the party of the first part, the same to be returned at the termination of his contract.

It is hereby mutually agreed by both parties hereto in consideration of the promises herein before set forth that should the party of the said second part at any time of times or in any manner fail to comply with covenants and agreements herein contained or any of them or any of the rules and regulations of the party of the first part, which are now or may hereafter from time to time be made, or should the party of the second part at any time or times be intemperate, immoral, careless indifferent or conduct himself in such a manner, whether on or off the ice, as to endanger or prejudice the interests of the party of the first part, or prove incompetent in the judgement of the party of the first part, then the said party of the first part hereunto shall have the right to discipline, suspend, fine or discharge the said party of the second part in such a manner as the said party of the first part shall deem fit and proper and in the case of fine imposed it is agreed by the party of the second part that he will pay the same or that same will be withheld as and for liquidated damages.

In order to enable the party of the second part to fit himself for the duties necessary under the terms of this contract, the said party of the first part may require the said party of the second part to report for practice or participate in such exhibition games as may be arranged by the said party prior to the opening of the league season but it is expressly agreed that the party of the first part shall pay to the party of the second part a salary for such games participated in at a pro rata rate of his regular monthly salary.

It is further agreed that if the said party of the first part should desire the services of the said part of the second part for any period of time after the date mentioned for the expiration of the term mentioned herein or which may be mentioned in any renewal hereof, said first party shall have the right to the same by paying compensation to the said second party for each game at a pro rata rate of regular weekly, monthly or season salary.

In witness whereof the said party of the first part has caused these presents to be signed by its officers thereunto duly authorized and the said party has affixed his hand and seal of the day and year first above written.

By ...............................................(Club President)


Player signs here  ...................................................
signature of second party

# *Appendix C*

## JOHN AMBROSE O'BRIEN

John Ambrose O'Brien, born in Renfrew, Ontario, May 27, 1885, was actively connected with hockey, having played junior, intermediate and senior at Renfrew, and later with University of Toronto.

In 1909 there existed only one professional league, the Eastern Canada Association. Renfrew team management decided they would like to join the ECHA but the application was refused. Undaunted by this, Mr. O'Brien decided to form a new league. So it was that in Montreal on December 3, 1909, the National Hockey Association was founded and was made up of Renfrew, Cobalt, Haileybury, the Montreal Wanderers and the Montreal Canadiens.

The M.J. O'Brien Trophy was for the championship of the NHA. It is now out of competition, was presented to the Hockey Hall of Fame by Ambrose O'Brien, and is on display. It was donated by the father of J.A. O'Brien.

He resided in Ottawa at the time of his death April 25, 1968.

Source: Hockey Hall of Fame, Toronto.

## FRED "CYCLONE" TAYLOR, O.B.E.

With a nickname befitting his style, Fred "Cyclone" Taylor was literally that on the ice. Reported as having scored a goal while skating backwards, Cyclone Taylor was brilliant in every phase of the game, early as a defenceman and then a forward.

He was born in Tara, Ontario, in 1885, but because he gained his early hockey fame in Listowel, many credit this town as his birthplace. From Listowel his hockey travels took him to Thessalon, Ont., and the famed hockey centre of years back, Portage La Prairie, Man. In 1906 he turned pro with Houghton, Mich., but moved on to Ottawa where he played in 1908 and 1909, Renfrew in 1910 and 1911, was out in 1912 but joined Vancouver in 1913. From 1913 to 1922 he played for the Vancouver Maroons and there accomplished some great scoring feats. In 18 games in the 1917-18 season he scored 32 goals while other similar schedules saw him rattle the nets for 24, 23 (twice) and 22 goals. He is credited with 194 goals in 186 league games and 15 goals in 19 playoff games.

He was honoured by the late King George VI with an O.B.E. for services during the Second World War.

He turned the sod for the Hockey Hall of Fame Building in 1960.

## LESTER PATRICK

The Silver Fox of professional hockey, Lester Patrick, wrote more than a page in the annals of hockey. After a fabulous career as a player, Lester rose to even greater heights in building pro hockey in Western Canada as well as in the NHL.

Born in Drummondville, Que., on Dec. 30, 1883, he started his hockey career with Montreal AAA in 1901. His first Stanley Cup trial was with Brandon, Man., in 1904, and two years later he joined the Montreal Wanderers to lead them to a Cup triumph over Ottawa in 1906. He stayed with the Wanderers for one more Cup win before moving to the B.C. coast with his family. His final amateur days were played with Kootenay.

The famed Renfrew Millionaires, in their one big try for the Cup, signed him for $3,000 with brother Frank getting $2,000. This led to the Patricks forming the Pacific Coast Hockey League and the building of arenas in which to play the games. It also led to two Stanley Cup triumphs by the Coast Leaguers, but in 1926 the Patricks sold their interests. Lester then came east to coach and manage the New York Rangers. Two more Stanley Cup victories were gained before he retired from the Rangers in 1946.

He died on June 1st, 1960.

## FRANK PATRICK

An outstanding defenceman and equally as outstanding as a keen student of hockey, Frank Patrick's name will long be recorded in the annals of hockey. Born in Ottawa in 1885, he learned his hockey in Montreal, becoming a star with the McGill University team.

He played with the famed Renfrew Millionaires along with brother Lester. Moving to Nelson, B.C., the Patricks decided to build not only a hockey league, but also arenas to house the teams. They climaxed their Pacific Coast Hockey League venture by winning the Stanley Cup in 1915. When the Patricks sold the league players to NHL interests, Lester came east, but Frank stayed in the west, though he later coached Boston and managed the Canadiens.

There are twenty-two pieces of legislation in the NHL Rule book which Frank introduced, the origination of the blueline being one.

He died in June of 1960.

## FRED WHITCROFT

One of the best in amateur and professional hockey was Fred Whitcroft, who made his fame early with Peterborough. He joined the monied ranks where he played for the famous Kenora Thistles in the March series against Montreal in 1907, when the Wanderers defeated Kenora to take back the Stanley Cup which the Thistles had won in January of the same year. Whitcroft went to Peterborough from Port Perry with his father in 1882 and played for the Peterborough Colts when they won the OHA junior championship in 1901. He was rover for the Peterborough intermediate team when they won the provincial title in 1906. Following this he went to Western Canada but was back in Kenora on a contracting job when club owner Thomas Hooper asked where he could get a good rover for his team. Whitcroft took the position. At the end of the season Whitcroft moved to Edmonton, and in 1908 was captain of the Edmonton team. He was described in those days as a good-sized man, very fast on skates, a dazzling stickhandler and a prolific scorer. In 1908 he scored forty-nine goals. Edmonton challenged for the Stanley Cup, went to Ottawa and lost two straight games. Whitcroft then went to Renfrew for a short time. He died in Vancouver.

## EDOUARD "NEWSY" LALONDE

Cornwall, Ontario, was the birthplace of several outstanding lacrosse and hockey players and one of the greatest was Edouard "Newsy" Lalonde, voted the outstanding lacrosse player of the first half-century and also one of the all-time greats of professional hockey.

Newsy was born in 1888 and acquired his nickname while working for a newsprint plant. He started his somewhat riotous pro career in 1905 with Cornwall and until 1935 was a dominant figure in the sport. His hockey travels took him to Toronto, Woodstock, Canadian Soo, Renfrew, Vancouver, Saskatoon and New York Americans. He wound up his active days as coach of theCanadiens.

As well as being a brilliant scorer, Newsy was also one of the roughest. His feuds with Joe Hall, when the latter was with the Quebec Bulldogs, used to fill the old Westmount Arena in Montreal.

During his active days he was five times scoring champion of various leagues, including the NHA, NHL and Pacific Coast League. In 365 games he scored 441 goals. In one year he netted 38 in 11 games, in another he scored 33 in 24 games, and with Vancouver scored 27 in 15 games. His scoring record leaves no doubt as to his ability.

## LORD STANLEY OF PRESTON, G.C.B.

Lord Stanley of Preston, G.C.B., was Governor General of Canada from 1888 to 1893, and it was during his final year in Canada he donated to the champion hockey club of the Dominion the famed Stanley Cup. The trophy, in 1893, cost just $50. And other than the original bowl there is little similarity between the trophy then and today's stately cup.

Until 1906 Canadian amateur clubs played for the Cup, but as professional hockey made its debut, the professionals took possession of the trophy and it travelled east to west for many years. When the Western Canada Hockey League disbanded in 1926, the NHL took over sole possession of the trophy.

From its original form of a rose bowl, the Stanley Cup now stands almost three feet high and grows each year as new winners are added. It is the oldest annual contested professional trophy in North America.

## ALFRED E. SMITH

There were many great hockey players with the name of Smith, but none perhaps better known that Alf Smith, who was born in Ottawa June 3, 1873, and died there on August 21, 1953.

His first team was the Ottawa Electrics of around 1890 and 1891. Then to the Ottawa Capitals, also amateurs. From there he played professional with Pittsburg. After one year, Alf returned to his home city to join the Ottawa Hockey Club.

In 1903-4-5 he captained and led the famed Ottawa Silver Seven to three world championships in a row. This was the first professional league in Canada.

In 1906 Alf was the moving spirit in breaking from the Silver Seven, and setting up Ottawa's second professional team. In the original league were the Ottawa Hockey Club (no longer called the Silver Seven), Wanderers, Quebec and the Montreal Shamrocks. In the newly formed Federal Hockey League were the Ottawa Senators, Smiths Falls, Brockville and Cornwall.

In 1909 Alf returned to Pittsburg where he captained and played for Pittsburg Athletic Club, this being his final season as a player.

Coaching then became his hockey activity and he was in charge for Ottawa Cliffsides, Renfrew, Ottawa, New York Americans, Moncton, and North Bay.

## SPRAGUE CLEGHORN

Sprague Cleghorn was born in Montreal in 1890 and played his hockey with the early greats of the game. Whenever experienced hockey men pick an all-time all-star team, Sprague can be figured to get his first or second-team mention on defence. His early hockey was with the New York Crescents in 1909-10, Renfrew in 1910-11, then the Montreal Wanderers 1912 to 1917.

In 1918 he was signed by the Ottawa Senators and was there three years. In 1921 he played for Toronto and then joined the Canadiens in 1922 and was with them four seasons, with the Stanley Cup again coming his way during the 1923-24 season.

His next and final club was the Boston Bruins, joining them in 1925 and remaining with the club until the end of the 1928 season. The next year the Bruins won their first Cup but Sprague, after approximately eighteen years of professional hockey, had finally hung up his gear.

Sprague was a product of Westmount, one of Montreal's elite areas, but he had no trouble fitting into the sometimes rough-and-tumble style of hockey played at that time, soon earning the respect of anyone who chose to tangle with him.

He died July 12, 1956, in Montreal.

# *Appendix D*

The Citizen Shield
*Courtesy The Fishenden Family*

The Renfrew Millionaires 1910 — photograph by A.L. Handford
*Courtesy Renfrew Recreation Committee, Harry R. Hinchley, Hockey Hall Of Fame*

The Renfrew River Hockey Team 1908-1909, Winners of the Citizen Shield, Champions Upper and Lower Ottawa Valley Leagues — photograph by A.L. Handford
*Courtesy Renfrew Recreation Committee, Thos. Fishenden Family*

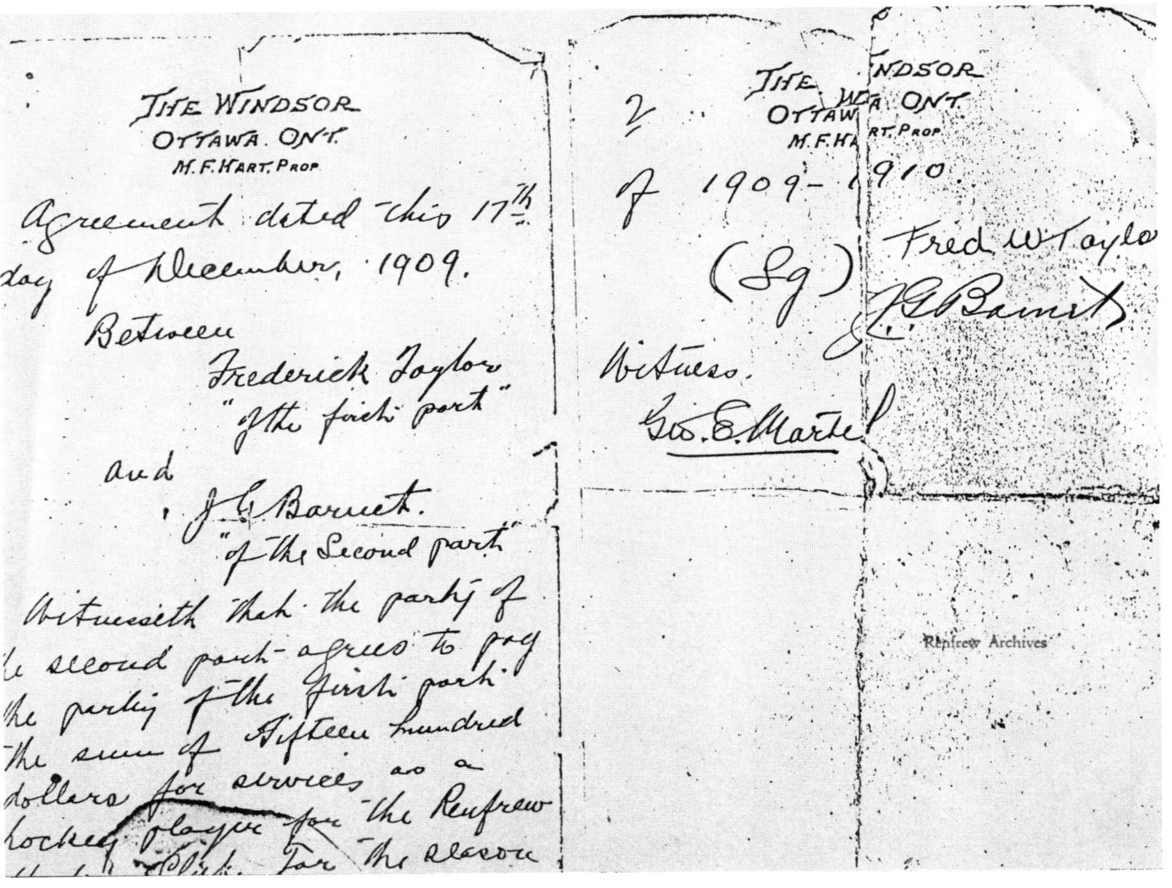

THE WINDSOR
OTTAWA. ONT.
M.F. HART, PROP.

Agreement dated this 17th day of December, 1909.

Between

Frederick Taylor
"of the first part"

and

J. G. Barnet.
"of the Second part"

Witnesseth that the party of the second part agrees to pay the party of the first part the sum of fifteen hundred dollars for services as a hockey player for the Renfrew [Hockey] Club. For the season

THE WINDSOR
OTTAWA. ONT.
M.F. HART, PROP.

2 ... of 1909-1910.

(Sg) Fred W Taylor
J. G. Barnet

Witness.
Geo. E. Martel

Renfrew Archives

Contract signed December 17, 1909 but subsequently voided by Cyclone Taylor.

O'Brien's Theater, Renfrew, Ontario

Memorial Plaque erected at O'Brien Park in 1967.

# *Endnotes*

## *Introduction*

1. *The Citizen*, Ottawa (29 December 1910).
2. ibid.
3. ibid.
4. ibid.
5. ibid.

## *Chapter One*

1. Young, *O'Brien*, p.60
2. *The Renfrew Journal* (23 April 1909).
3. *The Renfrew Mercury* (19 March 1909).
4. Roxborough, *The Stanley Cup Story*, p.12
5. ibid.
6. Cosentino, *A History of the Concept of Professionalism in Canadian Sport*, for a further discussion.
7. *The Star*, Toronto (14 December 1902).
8. ibid. (13 November 1906).
9. ibid. (16 December 1908).
10. *The Renfrew Mercury* (19 March 1909).
11. ibid. (15 March 1907).
12. Young, *O'Brien*, cited in.
13. ibid., for a further discussion.
14. *The Renfrew Journal* (27 December 1907).
15. ibid.
16. ibid.

17. ibid.
18. ibid.
19. *The Renfrew Journal* (30 December 1907).
20. ibid., cited in.
21. ibid. (30 January 1909).
22. ibid. (24 January 1908), cited in.
23. ibid. (7 February 1908), cited in.
24. ibid.
25. ibid. (11 December 1908).
26. Bennett, *The Story of Renfrew*, p.23
27. ibid., p.29
28. ibid.
29. ibid., p.24
30. ibid.
31. *The Renfrew Journal* (8 January 1909).
32. ibid. (15 January 1909).
33. ibid.
34. ibid.
35. ibid.
36. Bennett, *The Story of Renfrew*, p.98
37. *The Renfrew Journal* (23 April 1909).
38. ibid. (22 January 1909).
39. ibid. (26 January 1909).
40. ibid. (22 January 1909).
41. ibid. (5 February 1909).
42. ibid. (15 January 1909).
43. ibid. (22 January 1909).
44. ibid. (29 January 1909).
45. ibid. (22 January 1909).
46. ibid. (15 January 1909).
47. Bennett, *The Story of Renfrew*, p.30
48. ibid., p.91
49. *The Renfrew Journal* (22 January 1909).
50. ibid. (15 January 1909).
51. ibid. (22 January 1909).
52. ibid.
53. Selke, *Behind the Cheering*
54. The Renfrew Journal (15 January 1909).
55. ibid. (9 April 1909).
56. ibid. (19 March 1909).
57. ibid.

## Chapter Two

1. *The Gazette*, Montreal (15 November 1909).
2. <u>The Ottawa Evening Journal</u> (26 December 1909).
3. ibid.
4. Young, *O'Brien*, p.62, 63
5. ibid.
6. *The Globe*, Toronto (3 December 1909).
7. ibid.
8. *The Gazette*, Montreal (3 December 1909).
9. ibid.
10. ibid. (4 December 1909).
11. *The Citizen*, Ottawa (4 December 1909).
12. ibid.
13. ibid.
14. Whitehead, *Cyclone Taylor*
15. *The Globe*, Toronto (4 December 1909).
16. *The Gazette*, Montreal (6 December 1909).
17. ibid.
18. ibid.
19. Young, *O'Brien*, p.65

## Chapter Three

1. *The Citizen*, Ottawa (8 December 1909).
2. *The Globe*, Toronto (9 December 1909).
3. *The Renfrew Journal* (17 December 1909).
4. *The Globe*, Toronto (9 December 1909).
5. *The Ottawa Evening Journal* (9 December 1909).
6. *The Globe*, Toronto (9 December 1909).
7. *The Ottawa Evening Journal* (9 December 1909), cited in.
8. *The Gazette*, Montreal (15 December 1909).
9. ibid.
10. *The Renfrew Journal* (17 December 1909).
11. ibid. (10 December 1909), cited in.
12. ibid.
13. *The Ottawa Evening Journal* (11 December 1909).
14. *The Globe*, Toronto (15 December 1909).
15. *The Citizen*, Ottawa (10 December 1909).

16. *The Ottawa Evening Journal* (7 December 1909).
17. *The Gazette*, Montreal (14 December 1909).
18. Whitehead, *The Patricks*, p.65
19. ibid.
20. *The Ottawa Evening Journal* (18 December 1909).
21. ibid.
22. *The Renfrew Journal* (10 January 1910).
23. *The Citizen*, Ottawa (10 December 1909).
24. ibid.
25. ibid.
26. ibid.
27. *The Citizen*, Ottawa (17 December 1909).
28. ibid. (18 December 1909), cited in.
29. Coleman, *The Trail of the Stanley Cup*, p.576
30. *The Citizen*, Ottawa (18 December 1909).
31. *The Globe*, Toronto (23 December 1909).
32. ibid.
33. ibid.
34. *The Citizen*, Ottawa (18 December 1909).
35. ibid.
36. ibid.
37. ibid.
38. ibid.
39. ibid.
40. *The Ottawa Evening Journal* (20 December 1909).
41. ibid.
42. *The Citizen*, Ottawa (20 December 1909).
43. ibid.
44. ibid. (22 December 1909).
45. Whitehead, *The Patricks*, p.48
46. *The Gazette*, Montreal (22 December 1909).
47. *The Renfrew Journal* (17 December 1909), cited in.
48. *The Globe*, Toronto (24 December 1909).
49. *The Gazette*, Montreal (25 December 1909).
50. ibid. (27 December 1909).
51. *The Globe*, Toronto (29 December 1909).
52. *The Citizen*, Ottawa (27 December 1909).
53. ibid.
54. ibid.
55. *The Gazette*, Montreal (30 December 1909).
56. *The Renfrew Journal* (31 December 1909).
57. *The Globe,* Toronto (30 December 1909).
58. *The Gazette*, Montreal (30 December 1909).

*Frank Cosentino*

59. Whitehead, *Cyclone Taylor*
60. ibid., p.58
61. ibid., p.62
62. ibid., p.70
63. ibid., p.71
64. ibid.


## Chapter Four

1. Whitehead, *Cyclone Taylor*, p.114
2. *The Renfrew Journal* (30 November 1911).
3. ibid.
4. ibid.
5. ibid.
6. ibid.
7. *The Renfrew Mercury* (7 January 1910).
8. *The Citizen*, Ottawa (6 January 1910).
9. ibid.
10. *The Gazette*, Montreal (1 January 1910).
11. Whitehead, *Cyclone Taylor*, p.109
12. *The Renfrew Journal* (6 January 1910).
13. ibid.
14. ibid.
15. *The Gazette*, Montreal (3 January 1910).
16. ibid.
17. ibid. (5 January 1910).
18. ibid.
19. Whitehead, *Cyclone Taylor*, cited in, p.114
20. ibid.
21. Young, *O'Brien*, cited in, p.68
22. ibid., cited in.
23. *The Gazette*, Montreal (7 January 1910).
24. ibid.
25. *The Ottawa Evening Journal* (12 January 1910).
26. ibid.
27. ibid.
28. ibid.
29. ibid. (13 January 1910).
30. ibid. (12 January 1910).
31. ibid.

32. Young, *O'Brien*, p.68
33. *The Gazette*, Montreal (13 January 1910).
34. *The Renfrew Journal* (13 January 1910).
35. ibid.
36. Whitehead, *The Patricks*, p.72
37. *The Ottawa Evening Journal* (17 January 1910).
38. *The Globe*, Toronto (17 January 1910).
39. ibid.
40. ibid.

## Chapter Five

1. Young, *O'Brien*, cited in, p.63
2. *The Citizen*, Ottawa (17 January 1910).
3. *The Globe*, Toronto (20 January 1910).
4. ibid.
5. *The Renfrew Mercury* (21 January 1910).
6. *The Citizen*, Ottawa (20 January 1910).
7. *The Globe*, Toronto (20 January 1910).
8. ibid. (22 January 1910).
9. *The Citizen*, Ottawa (21 January 1910).
10. *The Globe*, Toronto (21 January 1910).
11. *The Citizen*, Ottawa (21 January 1910).
12. *The Renfrew Mercury* (10 January 1910).
13. ibid.
14. *The Globe*, Toronto (24 January 1910).
15. *The Citizen*, Ottawa (24 January 1910).
16. *The Globe*, Toronto (24 January 1910).
17. ibid.
18. *The Renfrew Mercury* (26 January 1910).
19. *The Globe*, Toronto (24 January 1910).
20. ibid.
21. ibid.
22. ibid.
23. *The Renfrew Mercury* (28 January 1910).
24. *The Citizen*, Ottawa (24 January 1910).
25. ibid.
26. ibid.
27. ibid. (28 January 1910).
28. *The Globe*, Toronto (28 January 1910).

29. ibid.
30. ibid.
31. *The Gazette*, Montreal (3 February 1910).
32. *The Ottawa Evening Journal* (5 February 1910).
33. ibid.
34. *The Citizen*, Ottawa (5 February 1910).
35. *The Ottawa Evening Journal* (5 February 1910).


## Chapter Six


1. *The Ottawa Evening Journal* (12 February 1910).
2. *The Renfrew Mercury* (24 March 1910).
3. *The Citizen*, Ottawa (11 February 1910).
4. ibid.
5. ibid.
6. ibid. (10 February 1910).
7. *The Gazette*, Montreal (11 February 1910).
8. *The Citizen*, Ottawa (12 February 1910).
9. *The Gazette*, Montreal (11 February 1910).
10. *The Ottawa Evening Journal* (14 February 1910).
11. ibid.
12. ibid.
13. ibid.
14. *The Citizen*, Ottawa (14 February 1910).
15. ibid.
16. ibid.
17. ibid.
18. ibid.
19. *The Ottawa Free Press* (14 February 1910).
20. ibid.
21. ibid.
22. *The Citizen*, Ottawa (15 February 1910).
23. ibid. (14 February 1910).
24. *The Renfrew Journal* (17 February 1910).
25. ibid.
26. *The Ottawa Evening Journal* (14 February 1910).
27. ibid.
28. ibid.
29. ibid.
30. ibid.

31. ibid.
32. ibid.
33. ibid.
34. *The Renfrew Journal* (17 February 1910).
35. ibid.
36. ibid.
37. ibid.
38. *The Citizen*, Ottawa (14 February 1910).
39. ibid. (15 February 1910).
40. *The Gazette*, Montreal (15 February 1910).
41. ibid.
42. *The Renfrew Journal* (17 February 1910).

## Chapter Seven

1. *The Ottawa Evening Journal* (16 February 1910).
2. ibid.
3. ibid.
4. *The Gazette*, Montreal (16 February 1910).
5. ibid.
6. ibid. (17 February 1910).
7. ibid.
8. *The Globe*, Toronto (18 February 1910).
9. *The Globe*, Toronto (21 February 1910).
10. *The Ottawa Evening Journal* (21 February 1910).
11. ibid.
12. ibid.
13. ibid.
14. Whitehead, *The Patricks*, p.76
15. *The Globe*, Toronto (23 February 1910).
16. ibid.
17. ibid.
18. ibid.
19. ibid.
20. *The Ottawa Evening Journal* (18 February 1910).
21. ibid.
22. *The Renfrew Journal* (24 February 1910).
23. ibid.
24. *The Renfrew Journal* (3 March 1910).
25. ibid.

26. ibid.
27. ibid.
28. ibid.
29. ibid.
30. ibid.
31. ibid.
32. ibid.
33. ibid.
34. ibid.
35. ibid.
36. ibid.


## Chapter Eight

1. *The Globe*, Toronto (26 February 1910).
2. ibid.
3. *The Gazette*, Montreal (9 March 1910).
4. Whitehead, *Cyclone Taylor*, p.115
5. Young, *O'Brien*, p.71
6. *The Renfrew Journal*, (10 March 1910).
7. ibid.
8. ibid.
9. ibid.
10. ibid.
11. ibid.
12. Whitehead, *The Patricks*, p.80
13. *The Globe*, Toronto (23 February 1910).
14. Coleman, *The Trail of the Stanley Cup*, p.190
15. Roxborough, *The Stanley Cup Story*, p.49


## Chapter Nine

1. *The Renfrew Journal* (17 March 1910).
2. ibid.
3. ibid.
4. *The Globe*, Toronto (19 March 1910).
5. ibid. (18 March 1910).

6. ibid.
7. *Evening Telegram*, New York (19 March 1910).
8. ibid.
9. ibid.
10. ibid.
11. *The Renfrew Journal* (24 March 1910).
12. ibid.
13. ibid.
14. *The Globe*, Toronto (21 March 1910).
15. ibid.
16. *The Renfrew Journal* (24 March 1910).
17. ibid.
18. ibid.
19. ibid.
20. Young, *O'Brien*, cited in, p.72
21. *The Renfrew Journal* (24 March 1910).
22. ibid.
23. ibid.
24. ibid.
25. ibid.
26. ibid.
27. ibid.
28. ibid.
29. ibid.
30. ibid.
31. ibid.
32. Bennett, *The Story of Renfrew*, p.302
33. ibid.
34. ibid.
35. ibid.
36. ibid.
37. ibid.
38. ibid.
39. ibid.
40. ibid.
41. ibid.
42. ibid.
43. ibid.
44. Drummond, *The Habitant*
45. *The Renfrew Journal* (24 March 1910).
46. *The Renfrew Mercury* (25 March 1910).
47.  ibid.
48. *The Renfrew Journal* (24 March 1910).

## *Epilogue*

1. Bennett, *The Story of Renfrew*, p.75
2. Coleman, *The Trail of the Stanley Cup*, p.206
3. Whitehead, *Cyclone Taylor*
4. ibid., p.197

# *Bibliography and Further Reading*


## *Newspapers*

*Edmonton Daily Bulletin*
*The Gazette,* Montreal, November 1909 - March 1910.
*Evening Telegram*, New York, March 1910.
*New York Times*, March 1910.
*The Evening Citizen*, Ottawa, December 1909 - March 1910.
*The Morning Citizen*, Ottawa, December 1909 - December 1910.
*The Ottawa Evening Journal*, November 1909 - March 1910.
*The Ottawa Free Press*
*Observer and Ottawa Valley Advocate,* Pembroke, January 1909.
*The Renfrew Journal*, 1908-1912.
*The Renfrew Mercury*, 1909-1910.
*The Globe*, Toronto, December 1909 - December 1910.
*The Star*, Toronto, December 1902 - December 1908.
*The Evening Telegram*, Toronto

## *Books*

Bennett, Carol, editor. *The Story of Renfrew*. Prepared for Heritage
     Renfrew. Renfrew: Juniper Books, 1983.
Bennett, Carol. *Valley Irish*. Renfrew: Juniper Books, 1983.
Coleman, Charles. *The Trail Of The Stanley Cup*. NHL: 1966.
Drummond, W.H. *The Habitant*. New York: G.P. Putnam & Sons, 1902.
Finnigan, Joan. *Some Of The Stories I Told You Were True*. Ottawa:
     Deneau, 1981.
Finnigan, Joan. *Giants*. Burnstown: General Store Publishing House,
     Inc., 1981.

*Frank Cosentino*

Finnigan, Joan. *Laughing All The Way Home*. Ottawa: Deneau, 1984.
Fitsell, J. W. *Hockey's Captains, Colonels and Kings*. Erin: Boston Mills Press, 1987.
Hockey Hall of Fame, Brochure. n.d.
McAuley, Jim. *The Ottawa Sports Book*. Burnstown: General Store Publishing House Inc., 1987.
Rooke, Patricia and R.L. Schell. *No Bleeding Heart*. Vancouver: UBC Press, 1987.
Roxborough, H. *The Stanley Cup Story*. Toronto: McGraw Hill Ryerson, 1964.
Selke, Frank. *Behind The Cheering*. Toronto: McClelland and Stewart, 1962.
Whitehead, Eric. *Cyclone Taylor*. Toronto: Doubleday, 1977.
Whitehead, Eric. *The Patricks*. Toronto:Doubleday, 1980.
Young, Scott and Astrid. *O'Brien*. Toronto: Ryerson, 1967.


## *Unpublished Papers*

Cosentino, Frank. "A History of the Concept of Professionalism in Canadian Sport." PhD Dissertation, University of Alberta, 1973.
O'Brien, Janet. "Contributions of Renfrew To Hockey History."
Graduate Essay, School of Physical and Health Education, Queen's University, 1974.
Schutt, John. "Renfrew Millionaires." Directed Studies essay, Department of Physical Education, Recreation and Athletics, York University, 1988.

*About
The Author*

Frank Cosentino is a well-known Canadian sports figure whose accomplishments include a CFL quarterback career from 1960 to 1969 with one year in Toronto, two years in Edmonton and seven years with the Hamilton Tiger Cats. He was a member of two Grey Cup teams. He continued his pursuit of athletics as head football coach for the University of Western Mustangs from 1970 to 1974. At present he is a professor in the Department of Physical Education, Recreation and Athletics at York University in Toronto where he instructs courses in the history of physical education, philosophy and issues in physical education, sports in Canadian life and football skills.

Mr. Cosentino was awarded an MA and a PhD in Physical Education from the University of Alberta and a BPE at McMaster University in Hamilton.

His published books include *Canadian Football: The Grey Cup Years*, *A History of Physical Education in Canada* with M.L. Howell, *Olympic Gold* with Glynn Leyshon, *Ned Hanlon, Lionel Conacher* with Don Morrow, *Winter Gold* with Glynn Leyshon, *A Concise History of Sport in Canada* with Morrow, Keyes, Simpson and Lappage, *A History of Physical Education* with Dinning, Jones and Malszecki, *The Renfrew Millionaires: Valley Boys of Winter 1910*, and *Not Bad Eh!: Great Moments in Canadian Sports History*.

Frank Cosentino was born on May 22, 1937, he is married to Sheila and has four children.

# *Other Sports Books from General Store Publishing House Inc.*

## Not Bad, Eh?
### Great Moments in Canadian Sports History

By Frank Cosentino

The standard by which other sports books will be measured! Canada's colourful sports history is documented through archival photographs and rich text. Thoroughly researched, this book covers great Canadian stories in both amateur and professional sports.

Nonfiction, 8 1/4" x 9 1/2", soft cover, archival photos

$19.95 plus $2.00 for shipping and handling


## Level Ice

By Bob Wake

Canadians are fascinated with the game of hockey. Bob Wake uses the game, its violence and emotion, as a backdrop to examine these same traits in his characters. Mr. Wake's writing has an old world elegance that makes the read a bit like going through an old family album and remembering simpler times.

Fiction, 4 1/2" x 7", soft cover

$9.95 plus $2.00 for shipping and handling

## The Ottawa Sports Book
**Vignettes From Ottawa's Sport History**

By Jim McAuley

The achievements of Ottawa's amateur and professional athletes and teams are relived in this exhaustively researched book by Ottawa sports-lover and columnist Jim McAuley. Experience the triumphs of Russ Jackson, Barbara Ann Scott, Frank "King" Clancy, Betsy Clifford and a host of others. Over 500 photographs, many never published before.

11" x 8 1/2", soft cover, 386 pages

$29.95 plus $2.00 shipping and handling

## O'Brien
**From Water Boy to One Million a Year**

By Scott Young and Astrid Young

This is the exceptionally well-researched life story of M.J. O'Brien, a famous early 20th century Ottawa Valley entrepreneur. M.J. owned five of the six hockey teams which would later become the NHL. From his humble beginnings as a water boy, he eventually oversaw the building of a large section of the Trans-Canada Railway.

Nonfiction, 5 1/2" x 8", soft cover

$11.95 plus $2.00 for shipping and handling

**To order send cheque or money order to:**
**General Store Publishing House Inc.**
**1 Main Street, Burnstown, Ontario, Canada  K0J 1G0**
**Telephone: (613)432-7697 or Fax: (613)432-7184**